COPYRIGHT © 2018 MALEEHA YOUSUF BERTIN
ALL RIGHTS RESERVED
Copyright Under Berne Convention
Registered at www.protectmywork.com
ACIP record for this title is available from the British Library

ISBN: 9781999337902

Formatted by: Muhammad Naseem

Contact details of the author are:
www.maleehabertin.com
www.maleehabertin.co.uk
Email: contact@maleehabertin.com

Follow me on instagram: Maleeha_yousuf_bertin

About the Author

Maleeha Yousuf Bertin is born and brought up in Pakistan and is now based in London with her husband.

She believes that the primary relationship one ever has is with themselves and this relationship with self can ultimately lead one to the truth about many aspects of life like relationships, God, and love.

Through this book, she is sharing wisdom on spirituality and relationships with her readers.

Acknowledgements

Having been raised in a Pakistani family with an unconventional father, I can't complete this book without thanking him, a man who had supported me all my life. Without his love and prayers, I would not be where I am today.

A special thanks to my parents for all their support all my life.

My wholehearted thanks also to my husband, Pierre-David Bertin (a revert to Islam), who has been a constant source of my inspiration. He believed in me and encouraged me to publish this book. Without his support, it would have been impossible. I remember while I was writing the dramatic scenes of the book, I was so lost in them I would often cry, and he would hold my hand and say, "You are very strong, my princess." At our second wedding anniversary, my book is finally being published. I hope our love keeps growing and we keep supporting one another in all our years together.

I would like to thank my family, my friends, and my secret admirers.

I would also like to thank all my teachers and my bosses who had immense faith in me and my capabilities to learn and grow.

A special thanks to my beautiful in-laws, who accepted me wholeheartedly, despite many cultural differences. A million thanks to grandma, my parents-in-law and the family for taking care of me and showering their love on me.

I would like to thank the editor of my novel and all other people who helped me with my publishing needs.

Thank you,
Maleeha Yousuf Bertin

Chapter 1

The Breakup

2010

The sun was shining brightly, and the temperature was 30 degrees Celsius. Abeera was standing in her balcony. She was short, skinny and fair. Her mind was disturbed by ill fortune. She pondered over many subjects. *I was in love with Daniyal. He was the 'man of my dreams.' I thought we would have a promising future. But the reality is so painful. What did I do to cause this? To be so hurt? Life is painful and full of disappointments. It felt like my joy would be eternal. He won my heart, but I am lonely and sad, wondering if there is a way one can fall in love and not get hurt. I wonder if eternal love still exists. Why do relationships hurt us? I want to die. I can't live without Daniyal who is so close to my heart and so close to my soul. What will I do without him?*

Abeera was heartbroken. This relationship was Abeera's, first love. It didn't last for long but left her devastated and in extreme mental suffering. Was it attraction or infatuation? Whatever it was, she couldn't take it anymore. But now it was time to move on. It was difficult for her to focus on her studies and work. Because of this relationship she had even stopped going out with her colleagues and university friends. She was still confused and very clueless about her life.

Abeera's breakup was not an extraordinary story – breakups are common – but for her, it was a life-changing experience, a blessing in disguise. It was the starting point from which all her learning and healing grew. Abeera's story and subsequent healing are beautiful, but to understand it fully, we first need to go back to the beginning of her relationship with Daniyal.

2009

Daniyal worked as a finance banker and she as a portfolio manager. They worked for the same bank. At the beginning of 2009, they met in an official meeting and immediately became friends.

After three months of their friendship, Abeera's university friend (Faheem) visited to see her family and expressed his desire to marry Abeera. She was looking for ways to avoid Faheem because he was just a friend for her even though he was good-looking, friendly, decent, had a good job and his family was also Punjabi like Abeera. But Abeera had never considered marrying him.

The next morning while driving to work she shared the proposal of Faheem with Daniyal on the phone. Daniyal became upset. Abeera didn't understand how serious he was in wanting to marry her. He immediately proposed to marry her. Abeera felt it was boring that Daniyal had proposed to her on the telephone. They had just met a few times in official meetings so from then on they dated regularly in the evenings. It quickly became a serious and committed relationship.

Now the next hurdle they had to overcome was to convince their families. In Eastern families, the man must bring his proposal to the girl's family. The girl's parents decide for her. The man's parents also have to agree. Both parents approve the marriage as a tradition and if they don't, then the couple has to get married on their own, through the court (where they register their marriage). But marriage in the court is very shameful for Eastern parents. Often the parents of both bride and the groom cut off ties with their children.

From that perspective, the situation was looking quite grim. Abeera belonged to a poor family; her parents had a blue-collar profession. However, she had a wonderful relationship with her father. He had always loved and supported Abeera so much so that her sisters were often jealous of her, especially her sister Savera. Abeera had two younger sisters and two elder sisters. Abeera's father had a small ladies' shoe shop in Lahore. He had another wife who was living in a village a few kilometres from Lahore. Abeera had never met her but her mother had told her about her. Abeera had two brothers. One was living in Dubai, Moiz. The other was living in America, Junaid. Junaid was Abeera's eldest brother. He had so many issues with the family that he never spoke to anyone. He left them when Abeera was 15 years old.

On the other side, in Daniyal's family, Daniyal was the only son. His mother had enormous expectations of him. In the East, some parents depend on their children and some even call it their 'right on their children'. Therefore, it is common that a man's mother would choose a bride for her son. If the son marries of his choice his wife might demand to live separately with him. Then he will have no choice but to leave his family.

Daniyal and his family were from Delhi, India, but had moved to Pakistan many years ago. His family had white-collar professions. They were a middle-class family but because of the profession of Abeera's parents; they thought of her and her family as low-class citizens. Unfortunately, someone had influenced Daniyal's family. With one bad experience, they made their perceptions. Daniyal explained to Abeera, "The Punjabi lady my cousin married was a working lady. She convinced my cousin to leave his parents and live separately with her. My cousin left his family and had little interaction with them. My mother thinks all Punjabi working girls are the same. My mother is terrified. She fears to lose me in her old age." Daniyal criticized and disrespected Abeera because of her parents' profession. Abeera had hated his criticisms and disrespectful words since the beginning of their relationship, but she disregarded them.

However the families' background were not the only clouds on the horizon. Daniyal's strange behavior on certain occasions was also a reason for concern. For example Daniyal sometimes said derogative things, such as, "Can't you study at a renowned university and only if you could speak better English?" Daniyal often corrected Abeera's English and gifted her an Oxford dictionary to improve her English.

Abeera's early education was from an English medium school, but her English was not very impressive. Studying at a renowned university was one of Abeera's dreams, but she couldn't afford it. She was studying at a local university with her own hard-earned money, but deep inside she wished she could study at a better university. She would often use words that didn't exist in the English language like 'genuinenism' and Daniyal would always criticize her severely.

Abeera would often wonder, *is criticism the only way to address issues in relationships? Is language a criterion for testing a person? How about all the other qualities required for a relationship: character, integrity, commitment, sincerity, honesty? Do these qualities matter anymore in relationships?*

She felt embarrassed by his poor standards. But this was also one of the core issues for Abeera. Since childhood, she had witnessed her parents being treated as low-class citizens. Their customers often disrespected, humiliated, and insulted her parents. Abeera was very sensitive. Persistent disrespect and humiliation only added to her frustration and hatred as she grew older. She developed a hatred for herself her family, and for being raised in this family. All these subjects were underlying issues for Abeera. She had never accepted her life, neither consciously nor subconsciously. Her parents' profession, their background, and their status were the biggest hurdles in her life. She hated their profession and was often ashamed to share the details of her parents' work with her friends and colleagues.

Abeera and Daniyal argued repeatedly about the perceptions that his family had of hers, "Just because your family had one bad experience with one Punjabi lady, does not mean that all Punjabi's are same!" she would say.

Despite this, Abeera was positive and wanted to meet Daniyal's family despite knowing about their prejudice. She felt she could change their perceptions by showing her unpolluted heart and love for their son.

Abeera had only heard love is powerful, love transforms and love needs nothing. And now she was wondering, *if this is love, what kind of lover would worry about his family's projections and perceptions?* "We are such a rigid, intolerant, and ignorant people. We need to raise our standards," she regularly told Daniyal. But Daniyal was not courageous enough to stand tall in front of his family.

Abeera couldn't see compatibility with Daniyal and his family's values, morals, and mindsets. But she hadn't seen many couples who were compatible, anyway. Most couples in her family would fight, argue, show disrespect to each other, etc.; day in and day out, and yet they continued to live together.

The biggest example was her mother. Abeera's father would repeatedly dominate, insult, and criticize her. But she had no courage to stand up for herself.

Abeera's parents had told her, "Marriages are made in heaven." But she would wonder, *if marriages are made in heaven, why are marriages not successful? Does that mean couples should live together even if they are not happy? If Daniyal is made for me, then will it work anyway? Will he show up on his knees? Or is there any criterion to the man of my dreams?*

Abeera found the courage to tell Daniyal, "We are two different people with two different backgrounds and mindsets. Your family will never approve of me." But every time she brought this up, either he would change the subject or doubt her love and trust, disrespecting her concerns and brushing off her words inconsiderately and carelessly. Whenever she expressed her dissatisfaction with their relationship, it would end up in arguments for the entire evening, and sometimes for days, they would stop communicating.

Despite being in this relationship, Abeera often felt unloved and isolated. She expected relationships to be joyful, loving, and magnificent. Someday a boy meets a girl, they fall in love, get married and live happily ever after. *Isn't this the dream of other girls too, to find the man of their dreams? What am I missing in this relationship? Is it wrong to express my discontent in a relationship?* She was repeatedly thinking.

Abeera had a few loving and caring friends. Some of them were her colleagues and some of them were her university and school friends. Amir was her best friend. He was educated, and intelligent. Abeera trusted him a lot. She went to him and shared her love story.

After listening to Abeera, Amir warned her, "Abeera, your lover is untrustworthy of what you have told me. I don't want to dishearten you, but I have my doubts. Please, Abeera. Be strong. Don't hurt yourself. In your case, your lover is not doing anything to prove his love. It is you who is running after him and wasting your time. A woman who is strong understands that no matter what the loss, it is far better than being neglected and disrespected. A woman who is weak compromises."

Abeera had multiple complex issues. This relationship had triggered her deep-seated fears. It puzzled her. She was unaccustomed to respect herself and was a stranger to being treated with respect in her relationships. She calmly replied, "Soon everything should be fine. I think you are losing patience. For a healthy relationship, you need time and patience." He whispered, "But the foundation should be right." That was not what Abeera wanted to hear.

She believed Daniyal was sincerely devoted to their relationship, "Amir, you don't get it," Abeera arrogantly replied. Amir's warning had only maddened her. She thought as he was very unfamiliar with the man she was talking about, his comments were absurd, "I will soon meet Daniyal's family and provide you with evidence of him being committed, devoted, and serious."

With each passing day, Abeera was getting increasingly involved in Daniyal. Her only focus was on him, mentally, physically and emotionally. Because of this, she struggled to work and study. Her performance was decreasing significantly at work and so was her interest in her studies. She would spend all day anxiously waiting for the evening to arrive and to be in his arms. He was like a drug she needed every day.

In the beginning, they met once a day and then they would meet twice a day. For breakfasts and evenings. Not a day would pass without them seeing each other. Abeera became so obsessed that to imagine life without him was already frightening.

After four months

As Daniyal was showing no seriousness, she suggested that he should introduce her to his family. In the beginning, it looked as if he was disinterested in doing so, but finally, on one evening, he introduced Abeera to his older sister at a restaurant.

The following day.

Daniyal told Abeera that you impressed my sister. But Abeera could feel that his sister didn't approve of her and Daniyal's feedback about her was inaccurate. Abeera remained quiet and refrained from making a judgement.

Now that Abeera had met Daniyal's sister, Abeera suggested that he should send a formal proposal. She was actively pursuing the relationship while he was silently observing and only following her instructions.

Finally, Daniyal convinced his family. They were ready to meet Abeera and her family, but only to have a dialogue over a cup of tea, not to come with a proposal of marriage. After a few days, Daniyal visited her family with his sister and parents. Abeera's two older sisters with their husbands and her parents attended the meeting. Both families were not convinced with this relationship and needed more time to take a decision.

A month passed.

It was EID, September 2009, one of the most important Muslim religious occasions. Abeera's mother sarcastically told her, "If Daniyal and his family were serious about the relationship, they would have visited us today, or, at the bare minimum, they would have sent sweets as a token of love."

Abeera abruptly replied, "Mom, don't worry. They're extremely occupied. I met him yesterday. He apologized. We went shopping for EID, and I really enjoyed. Look, Daniyal bought a lovely present for you. Isn't it nice of him?" Silently observing what her daughter had shown her, Abeera's mother said nothing and left the room. Abeera followed her mother into her room and continued, "Mom, he will convince his family soon, in just a matter of a few days. Mom, please try to understand. He needs more time."

Abeera had lost herself in him. Her mother could clearly see it, but she remained quiet. Abeera was happy outside, but inside herself, she was extremely worried but she ignored the reality of her inner self. Instead, she enjoyed the gifts Daniyal bought for her and the times they spent together. She and Daniyal had spent birthdays, EID, and many special occasions together. They would speak for hours and hours on the phone. She would barely sleep, and all day they would exchange messages and emails.

Another month passed.

Daniyal explained to Abeera, "My mother is afraid we might get married secretly, and that's why my family has visited your family. But I need more time to convince my family to bring in a proposal."

Abeera's family continued to be not convinced with this relationship either; nonetheless, they were ready to support Abeera with her decision. She was pressurizing Daniyal to get married to her with or without his parents.

Abeera waited for a few days but Daniyal did not take any decision. With each passing day, she was becoming depressed and losing her patience. She did not understand how long she should wait. She had given more time to this relationship than she wanted.

After a lot of deliberation, she decided to test Daniyal's love for her and invited him for tea at her place. Daniyal came to see Abeera and her family. After having tea, Abeera's father, in his commanding voice told Daniyal, "You have two weeks to convince your family, or otherwise I will get Abeera married to someone else. Do you agree?"

Daniyal nodded.

Her father asked again, "If you want more time, please tell me."

He nodded again, "I completely agree, Sir."

Abeera and Daniyal kept meeting regularly during the two weeks. She reminded him about his commitment of two weeks, but he gave her excuse after excuse.

THE GIRL WHO LOVED HERSELF

Two weeks later.

Daniyal left the city and went to Islamabad to attend his sister's wedding. Abeera called him a few times before midnight. He didn't take her calls.

Fuming with anger Abeera waited for three hours, but Daniyal did not call her back. Abeera accepted the result. The decision she should have taken long ago. Abeera told herself, *if he can't keep his commitments, what's the point of this relationship?* She was now ready for all the consequences.

She sent him a text message. "It's over. Never call me again."

Within a few minutes of her message, he called her repeatedly, about 50 times that night, but Abeera took none of his calls. *If he loved me, why did he not keep his commitment?*

He angrily sent her a text message. "Why aren't you answering my calls?" Abeera replied again, "It's over."

Tears were flowing from her eyes. She cried the whole night, asking for help from God. *Only God is my witness of what I am going through and only God can free me from this hurt.*

So many emotions were running through Abeera's mind. She committed to moving on. She was very headstrong, but she felt weak thinking, *how does one fall in love and not lose themselves? Making a choice is always difficult, yet short-term pain is better than long-term unhappiness.*

The following months were full of pain. She missed all the beautiful times they had spent together—the breakfasts, the evening teas, and the walks in the park. Her heart was aching from her shattered dream.

Abeera was broken-hearted, and her ties with Daniyal were broken. A page of her life turned. She cried for hours and hours and thought her life would end and she would die. Depression, anxiety, and sleepless nights affected her physical body as she could barely eat.

Her family became extremely upset. Every night her mother would ask her to eat, but she would refuse.

She only had two options: either go back to Daniyal and apologize or forget him. Both options were immensely painful. Should she let go of her self-respect or let go of him? She was at a crossroads. Everyone has certain boundaries and there are things they can't tolerate. Letting go of her self-respect was non-negotiable for her. She had allowed no one to disrespect her at least knowingly.

But, it wasn't a stroll in the park. Daniyal called her frequently and sometimes even daily. It only aggravated her discomfort. Abeera didn't respond to Daniyal's calls, though every time he would call, she would cry. The more she tried to forget him, the more bitterly disappointed she felt by his calls.

Another month passed.

Disheartened, and disappointed by her own mistakes, Abeera had to confront her deepest fears, leading her to accept the past she was escaping from. She had not fully recovered from the emotional pain, but it helped her come to terms with herself, her education, her parents' profession, and her family's background—which she had never accepted.

Every time she missed him she would remind herself: I am much more worthy than the way he treated me. He disrespected me many times. I deserve to be with someone who respects me, not only with his words but with his actions. Not only saying he commits but also proving it. Not only claiming he is sincere but also enabling me to see his sincerity. Besides, if a man can't keep his word, how would I ever trust him, even if I end up getting married to him?

Daniyal sent her an email after a month trying to reach her.

From: Daniyal
Date: Dec 15, 2009 11:14
Subject: Love you
To: Abeera Shaikh

Dear Abeera,

This is my letter to you. You know I have been trying hard to see you face to face and made several calls to you. Though email is not my style, I want to sleep without the thought of missing you. I don't want to feel the heartache of hearing your name or things that remind me of you, and I want to know the reason you did what you did.

I want to be strong again. I want to fight and conquer. This is what I am doing right now. I know I will win this battle. I will beat the demons inside my heart and head. Because I am worth it. I am worth every goddamn thing that the world has to offer. I am changing; I am growing; I am evolving. Yeah, I was a diamond in the rough, but my issues are the last remaining bit of dirt that keeps me from shining like a star.

I am not mad at you; I hold nothing against you. I love you. Well, I think I do. I don't know how much you have changed as a person and in your character. Maybe I don't even like you anymore. Well, I believe there's still an echo of what you once were.

What happened to you? Your father was sitting on a ticking bomb. It doesn't work that way. You, instead of being on my side, send me a text that it's over. What kind of love is that? If you loved me, you could have waited for me. You knew I was out of town at my sister's wedding. You could have waited for another few days. I was busy, my family was busy. I had no time to speak to them.

And your brother-in-law—he looks so weird. The poor sister that got married to him; my family didn't like him. I have been trying hard to convince my family, but you have not supported me. You should have stood by my side.

I realized it takes two to tango. Even though my heart was in it from the beginning, yours was not. I could face every major storm on the way, but you were too delicate to put your feet on the ground and understand. I don't blame you. We BOTH needed change to let us work.

You have wasted so much of my time for all this. You are such a waste of time. I deserve better treatment from you.
Goodbye.
Daniyal

Abeera was feeling better now but was far from over him completely. She read the confusing email. The message was ambiguous. She went to Amir and asked him to translate the email. Maybe he could understand what the message was?

"What does he want? Is he apologetic? Does he want a chance? Is he willing to move on? Is he willing to make things work? Should I wait? How long? How long am I supposed to wait? Is it even worth giving him a chance?" Abeera despaired.

It also confused Amir like her, "The message is very ambiguous. I had told you Abeera before that you can't trust him. He doesn't know what he wants. He is still willing to take his chance and see if you want to stick to him."

Abeera got angry with this interpretation, "It is not a joke. He thinks he can walk into my life when he wants and walk over me when he pleases. I have had enough of this and I won't be giving him any more chances."

Amir was happy that Abeera was finally willing to move on. He replied, "I would advise you ignore this email."

A few days passed.

She cried day in, day out. She was no longer dependent on Daniyal or waiting for his formal proposal. However, his email had completely baffled her. She had not expected him to drag her family into it or degrade her love once again.

Abeera for the first time realized that Daniyal was not tall, young, or handsome. He was old, short, dark, and boring. His odd glasses looked terrible on him, but she had never mocked him about them.

She had already placed him on a high pedestal, just because he was making more money than her and because of his education.

Abeera was ingrained with this belief since her childhood "Woman is weak. She needs a man to support her, provide for her, protect her, and without a man she is incomplete."

Abeera's standards were so low. She considered nothing else and accepted his proposal. But now she wanted to take a stand for herself. Now she wanted to decide for herself. Now was the time she wanted to prove her self-worth.

A relationship might work, or it might fail, but in this process, she had lost herself in him. Some of her friends were having fun dating, but she was struggling with her first love.

One thing Abeera had gotten from this relationship was the ability to *question*. She now questioned everything. Though, she wasn't sure if she would ever get answers to all her questions. This approach differed from her childhood when her family instructed her not to ask too many questions. Women should stay quiet, just like Abeera's mother, who had never raised her voice or voiced her distress, even when inside herself she was very unhappy. Abeera had seen her mother crying secretly several times.

Daniyal hadn't stopped calling Abeera. This time when he called her. He asked her to meet. Abeera accepted because she wanted to confront him.

The following day. They met at a coffee shop. The night before and during the day she thought about all the questions she wanted to ask. More than anything she thought of how angry she was.

She took a printout of his email and drove to the coffee shop. When he approached her, she stepped out of the car. She looked gorgeous in her creamy white long shirt, beige trousers, and delicate sandals topped off with her lovely sunglasses.

They entered the coffee shop. He ordered an orange juice for himself. He offered Abeera a drink, but she replied, very angrily, "I am not here to drink. I am here to talk about your stupid email!" Without a pause, she continued, "Who the hell do you think you are?"

She took the printout of his email from her handbag.

"What? You printed my email?" he said in astonishment.

"Yes, just as you see it!" Abeera replied.

She exploded, "How dare you write this email about me, my love and my family! What was more important? Your sister's wedding, that happened in a few days out of nowhere, and me and my family? Your family is important, your sister's wedding is important. I get that, but what about me? Is there a place for me in your life? I suppose not. Then why all this drama about love and a relationship? If you can't keep your word, your commitments, what the hell are we doing here? I don't get it! You are very discourteous. My father expected a call from you, at least a phone call to inform him you were busy. I'm sorry; I won't tolerate this anymore. It's over. Please stop chasing me. I'm not here to mend this relationship and give you a second chance. And you, what did you write? That I was wasting your time? No, sorry, let me correct you. It was silly of me to have wasted my time with an asshole like you!"

He tried to calm her down, "I love you. Please don't raise your voice. This is a public place, there are people around us. For heaven's sake, listen."

But Abeera didn't care.

"Don't you dare say 'I love you' again? A man who cannot respect himself cannot respect anyone else. And love without respect doesn't exist. Learn self-respect first." She picked up her handbag and continued, "Never call or write to me again. This is over!"

She headed out and got into her car.

He immediately rushed out of the coffee shop, followed her, and tried to engage in conversation with her. But she completely ignored him and drove off.

Abeera arrived at Amir's house. She unrestrainedly indulged in smoking and drinking to fill the void within herself and the intolerable pain she was going through. She had never consumed alcohol or smoked before. She didn't realize how potent the effects of alcohol could be. Amir told her, "People use alcohol to reduce pain, and when the effect is over you face the same reality, the reality of your life, with all of its pain and sorrow."

She struggled to accept that her relationship was over even though she herself had initiated the breakup. She had such high hopes and high expectations from her first love.

For a few months, she remained in denial, continually drinking and smoking. She became addicted rather than trying to heal.

Abeera was regularly talking to Amir. Amir explained to her a few times, "Denial is a common characteristic of alcoholism. Alcoholics will deny they have problems in life. They may not even realize how serious their drinking habit is. Denial is a dangerous place to be. It keeps you away from getting the help you need."

Every time Abeera would drink, she would cry, *my emotions are foolish. I can't believe why my heart cries for him, who didn't care for me. Why am I so weak? I felt I was strong enough to let go.*

2010

Abeera developed a terrible pain in her back. The colleagues rushed her to the hospital. But apparently, there was no specific reason for the pain. The next time she called Amir, he explained to her, "Our body is a tool, our body sends us signals, and our thoughts affect our bodies. Negative thoughts about any subject are a resistance to healing. When we go to the root cause of our body's imbalances, we get the power to heal. Our bodies are energies. There is a link between emotional pain and physical pain. Our work is to release the blockage of energies by identifying the root cause."

Abeera went through the transition while the back pain took time to heal completely. She was no longer resisting and escaping from all the issues that came to her mind through the breakup.

She questioned all the criticism she had for herself, which Daniyal had only confronted her with unconsciously. She went into a new phase of life, questioning herself, her fears and her beliefs.

Abeera realized the purpose of some relationships is to bring unhealed parts of ourselves into our conscious state and make us aware of them. These relationships shed light on the unresolved issues that are stored in our bodies. If we accept them, we allow ourselves to heal and we free ourselves from the negative baggage. This is an important step to recognizing when one has taken the inward journey.

She had an opportunity to eagerly and decisively use her breakup to heal herself and live a happy and contented life.

The doctor had advised her to do exercises and go for physiotherapy. She took regular classes of physiotherapy and daily evening walks. Her general state of mind remained a state of high confusion, but she was working with herself, pondering over many subjects, and making peace with the different aspects of her life.

Her eldest brother-in-law, Ameen, who cared about her, was lining up potential candidates for her to engage with and decide for marriage. Ameen was not only Abeera's brother in law but also her well-wisher. He admired her immensely and wanted her to get settled. He was impressed with Abeera's hard work and had always supported her.

Abeera was terrified, and on a constant emotional roller coaster ride, with both highs and lows, looking for stability.

A few days later an incident happened at work:

Abeera was forced to stay late at work until midnight. Though, she never

THE GIRL WHO LOVED HERSELF

had an issue with staying late but a tragedy had happened. While her father was relighting the geyser, he caught fire and received burns on his legs.

Abeera's older sister called and told her what happened.

Abeera requested her manager several times to allow her to go home early, but he refused, as it was the end of the month. Everybody was falling below targets. At lunch break, Abeera rushed to the home and requested Ameen to take care of her father. Ameen took her father to the doctor and got him the treatment.

That day she reached home late and got embarrassed as her sister's in-laws were visiting to see her father.

Abeera would always put others above her. Even though she had tried to arrive home early. This incident helped her to stand up for herself. In the past, she wouldn't have done anything. This time she decided to make a complaint against her manager to the Human Resource Manager.

The next morning.

Abeera went straight to the HR head's office. She couldn't help her tears rolling down her cheeks because of the inconsiderate behavior of her manager. The Human Resource Manager was very compassionate and apologetic to her. He asked the manager to see him. After some discussion with the manager, they asked Abeera if she would mind being transferred to a branch at a better location, closer to her residence with easy parking facilities. The branch Abeera was working in was in the middle of the city and in the night it was difficult for a female to get to the parking. The parking was arranged at 2 kilometers from the branch in a vacant plot having no electricity. The Human Resource Manager recognized that Abeera should work for a branch where she could feel more comfortable. Abeera agreed and got transferred to a branch at a fantastic location, close to the house where she lived with her parents, and with easily available parking.

The manager in the new branch was friendly and cooperative, and the area was beautiful. She enjoyed the new branch. She would arrive home early, go for a walk, and attend yoga classes during the weekend. She made new friends and would sit on park benches just to reflect and feel what she had inside herself. For the first time, she could witness her thoughts and feelings. It was a very new and unique experience for her.

On the other hand, Daniyal had not stopped calling her, but she did not answer his calls.

However, she had still not given up on the "man of her dreams."

A week later, she saw her teacher in the parking lot of her branch. She immediately went to her, greeted and confessed:

"Ma'am, I am upset."

"Oh darling! What happened to you?"

"I had a breakup," Abeera replied, without hesitating.

"When?"

"It's been a few months, eight months, now." Abeera couldn't speak and burst into tears.

The teacher nodded in surprise. "What? Eight months? Move on and make peace with your past. You're stronger than that. You can't live your life in the past, move forward!"

With that, her teacher left the parking lot, without Abeera having a chance to thank her.

Abeera was this teacher's favorite student. She admired Abeera. Abeera was a role model for her teacher. She appreciated Abeera's intelligence and the way she would carry herself, so much so that for all the question-and-answer sessions in the class she would wait for Abeera's answers, before others. She would even call Abeera her *'Miss Perfect'*.

When Abeera was in tenth grade. Her principal made her the head girl in her school. She was the class representative in her college, and her campus director had even offered her a job at the university. Abeera's school principal had also given Abeera a scholarship for two years and she really adored Abeera.

But in all these years, Abeera had never been grateful to anyone. She had never appreciated people who admired her.

Now she wanted to show sincere gratitude to all these people. The next day, she called her teacher and the principal and thanked them for their love and appreciation for her.

But Abeera was still wondering what 'peace' was.

Later that same evening, she received a call from Daniyal. She picked up the phone, and, without greeting him, she said, "Don't you get it? I don't want to talk to you anymore. Can you stop calling me? What do I have to do to make you understand that I have moved on?"

That was the last call Abeera ever received from him, and he never called her again.

In the evening when Abeera called Amir, he asked Abeera to let go and explained to her, "Letting go is not giving up. It simply means you are strong enough to accept this moment. And wise enough to have faith for whatever comes your way."

In another few days

She had to take her annual leaves from work.

She travelled to Dubai and spent her holidays with her brother Moiz.

In Dubai, Abeera looked around bewildered, in awe, staring for a long time at the tall towers. Her experience forced her to clear the inner turmoil and discover the lessons waiting for her. With each passing day, she felt more confident with her lessons learned. She sensed calmness arising within her. This was the 'peace' her teacher had talked about.

A few days far away from the daily routine and the hustle and bustle of life, Abeera really enjoyed being with herself and her brother. Abeera called Amir and told him that she was at peace, as now, she had accepted her background, past and herself for the first time.

Abeera was now coming back to Pakistan with her learned lessons.

Lessons we can learn from Abeera:

Acceptance is to accept people, circumstances and events as they are in this moment. If we negate our experiences, we create negativity within us, and if we accept, we learn and grow.

Acceptance is also to accept one's background, one's family and one's past.

With acceptance comes peace and clarity. We cannot move further unless we make peace with the present, right now, right here.

Abeera decided for herself: my happiness matters the most and I will always choose that which makes me happy and I will not accept less than a safe and respectful relationship.

Abeera realized: That the relationship had brought her own issues into her conscious world, to mirror how she felt about herself.

Abeera realized: It was her lack of love for herself that made her continue to be in this relationship with Daniyal.

Abeera learned that if she had loved herself, she would give herself nothing but the best.

Abeera learned that a person who loves you will love you the way you are and will not criticize or mock you.

Abeera asked herself the following questions: How many times have you allowed people to hurt you and never had the courage to get over the relationship? How many times have you been in a relationship because of your fears? How many times have you hated yourself for lying to yourself? How many times have you acted on beliefs ingrained since your childhood? When was the last time you raised your standards?

Abeera realized: That no matter where you are and what life situation you are in, you can always take control of your life, provided you don't give up on yourself.

Experiences build perceptions, and perceptions can soon become beliefs. It then becomes a cycle, a cycle where the same experiences keep repeating in your life.

Abeera realized that relationships do not hurt us; it is our expectations from them that hurt us. If we keep holding others responsible for our hurt, we will never learn and grow.

Chapter 2

The Transition

2011

After Abeera returned from Dubai, she went for Pilgrimage to Saudi Arabia with her parents.

Abeera was very excited. She had read that the first time you gaze at the 'Khana Kaaba' (the House of God) and make any prayer, God will answer them. She tried hard to learn a few prayers to make at her first gaze.

But the first time she saw the House of God, she could hardly remember anything and she burst into tears. She had only seen the image in pictures and on television. All she could ask was: "God, please forgive me."

For the rest of the week, all she did was cry, and ask for forgiveness from God.

In childhood, Abeera's father did not allow Abeera and her sisters to communicate with boys. But as they grew and worked, her father ultimately allowed them to communicate with boys. This had only created contradictions in Abeera's life. *Do devoutly religious and God-fearing women never talk to men?* She wondered.

The week was soon over and Abeera had received no sign from God. *Maybe God is angry with me*, she thought. She offered several prayers but received no sign from God.

She wondered, *but how does God speak to us? Is coming to the 'House of God' enough to get His attention? What must I do to know if God has forgiven me?*

Abeera's mother told her, "God is very near to everyone, and God answers every prayer." So, according to that, God must have answered Abeera by now.

"But what does one need to do to hear God?" She asked her mother. Her mother replied, "God created humans only to obey Him, please Him, and be fearful of Him. God is only for pious people, for people who pray five times each day, who perform fasts, give charity, and recite the Holy Book."

Abeera was sad and felt guilty. God was not for her according to the description her mother gave her.

She and her parents had performed the pilgrimage; now they were heading back home.

In the evening they reached home, Abeera went to Amir and told him she was very guilty. Amir explained to her, "Guilt eats you up, and people can have severe illnesses from it. Guilt can't erase what you did, but by accepting it, you can free yourself from guilt."

Abeera replied to him, "I have accepted my breakup; I have accepted that I wronged myself, and I have cut off all ties with him."

He replied, "Good, change starts from acceptance."

Abeera embarked on a quest to reclaim herself, to turn the breakup into an opportunity for renewal and self-discovery, to expand and develop new interests rather than pitying herself. She tried many things and reconnected with old friends.

She developed a new routine for her life and prioritized herself to design a joyous life. Sometimes she would go to a spa and have a massage, pamper herself with facial, manicure, and pedicure; and other times she would read books and write about her feelings, grievances, moods, and happiness.

Soon Abeera became busy with her routine life. One day when she walked to her car she was dreadfully shocked, *"What! Is this my car?"* She checked the license plate to identify it. She laughed inside. It was her car!

For the first time, she noticed the marvelous painting in her room, full of the colors of the rainbow. It felt like the light was shining through the painting.

Everything felt alive. Everything felt new and beautiful. She was transforming and that is why she felt this.

This transition led her to many realizations. After 26 years spent hating herself, she finally realized that all she was missing was self-love. Many of her friends admired her petite figure and her tiny, beautiful feet but she had spent all her life hating herself. She didn't know that in some cultures, 'foot binding' was the custom of applying tight binding to the feet of young girls to change the shape and size of their feet. Her naturally small feet were an absolute gift.

While she was making her discoveries. It was now her graduation day.

She wanted to be independent. Her father had taught her that, "Women should stand on their feet to face any calamity that might come into their lives. Women should be able to differentiate between good and bad. Working and educated women become good housewives, mothers, and daughters. To pursue your dreams, to find a dream man, to find a dream job, the fundamental thing was to get an education."

Throughout the preceding five years, all the university work, long classes, stressful studying and sleeplessness had paid off. Standing in the queue all day, she couldn't wait to walk across the stage to get her degree. Many thoughts were racing through her mind. *You believe you can perform in the big world, and that the future might not be as scary as you thought. You can make your family and friends proud of you for reaching this milestone.*

Abeera was the first daughter in her family who had earned an MBA. It was an emotional occasion for her. She walked onto the stage to receive her degree. Now, she had earned the right to be called a 'master'.

Today was the day for Abeera to celebrate. A celebration without drinking seemed inadequate to her. It's what all her friends did. She had many friends,

THE GIRL WHO LOVED HERSELF

but one common practice for all of them was to drink, smoke, and sleep around. Some men brought women with them who they called 'friends', and some would introduce each other in the group— even married men. And after drinking, eventually, these 'friends' would sleep together. Abeera hated sex and wondered, "Is this what people call 'friends with benefits' in the West, or is it another form of prostitution?"

Abeera would only go to these group of friends to drink and enjoy her own company.

A year after her breakup.

Abeera got attracted to a handsome, graceful and good-looking guy, Samar. She met him in an official meeting with her boss. His office was at a beautiful location on the beach front: a marvelous combination of beauty and richness, the perfect picture of her imagination. During the first meeting, Abeera felt lost and daydreaming. *Ah! Love at first sight.*

Samar belonged to one of the high classes of Pakistan and was fluent in English with a lovely accent. He looked humble, confident, and composed.

After what had happened in her last experience, Abeera had not expected that love would come to her so quickly. Anxiously waiting for the man of her dreams, she wanted to take her chances and test her fate once again.

After the meeting, she sends Samar a message praising his office, "Your office is exquisite. I took pictures to share with my friends. I hope you don't mind."

Samar replied, "Sure. I don't mind."

From that day they exchanged messages regularly.

Abeera felt he might be in love with her.

In a matter of days, they became friends. Yet Samar stayed reserved.

Abeera felt like a teenager experiencing a first crush. All she would do is think of Samar throughout the day. She tried to force herself to stop thinking about him, but she would even dream about him. The more she wanted to hide, the more he would bump into her. It was hard to get him off her mind. Her confusion and desperation only increased. *Why would I attract him into my life? He is filthy rich, gorgeous, and must have a queue of beautiful women chasing him. Why would he choose me?*

One day, she went for the aerobics class; she saw Samar there, but she didn't have the courage to walk up to him and strike up a conversation as they only talked and sent text messages on the phone.

Later in the night, she asked Samar, "What did you do in the evening?"

He replied, "Gym."

Abeera inquisitively asked, "The fitness club?"

Samar replied, "Yes."

She had seen Samar sitting in the reception area and they both had gazed at each other for a few seconds. But Samar ignored her. However, she quickly changed the subject. She felt that maybe Samar was reluctant to open himself to her.

A few days later she saw Samar again, on the street, waiting at a traffic signal with his friends.

Abeera became more inquisitive. Were all these signs of the man of her dreams?

The unexpected meeting at the beginning, the inexplicable feeling of shyness, then bumping into each other, not once, not twice, but several times.

Abeera became more curious each day. She would wait all day long to talk to Samar in the evening, though, she didn't want to lose herself in him and hurt herself as before. So she continued going out with her friends and focused on her work and studies.

She gave Samar some signs while they were chatting.

She wrote a poem for him and shared it with him, but she didn't mention that the poem was for him. It went like this:

While the rain was pouring and my heart was dancing

I couldn't stop looking around for you around
I couldn't stop screaming your name inside
Your name and my name,
Together they both look so complete

I felt you so close to my heart
You aroused every inch of me
I was now losing control over myself
There I was lying with you, in your arms you held me

The world was so different there,
So peaceful and comforting
As if that's the place I will stay forever
So many wild thoughts running over my mind

THE GIRL WHO LOVED HERSELF

My biggest desires were coming true
I felt heaven, heaven on earth
And I could see a new life, full of love
It's wonderful to be in your arms

While the rain was pouring and my heart was dancing

Abeera was very excited. She went to her mother, "Mom, everything should be fine from here on." Her mom asked her why. But she decided not to share anything more. Perhaps she hadn't learned how to express her feelings and intuitions. She intuitively felt that everything would change and would be for the best.

The next day.
Samar invited Abeera for coffee. She was very excited and went over to see him, dressed in her light pink, beautiful Eastern dress with high heel shoes, lovely bag, topped with unique earrings.

She searched for a parking place, parked her car and went inside the coffee shop. Samar was waiting for 10 minutes.

Abeera, after saying, "Hi, sorry I'm late," sat down on the chair in front of Samar.

She felt very nervous but quite excited to see Samar for the first time outside the office, feeling she was on cloud 9.

After ordering coffee for them Samar asked, "How have you been?"

"Great," she answered and continued without pause, "So you are the owner of the big company. Gosh!"

"No, don't you know who I am?" he replied, with an unexpected smile.

"What? You're the man who owns the big company, no?"

"No, you are mistaken. I don't. My grandfather gave it to my father and his brothers that's all."

"So what? It is still your family business," she eagerly replied, brushing his comment off.

"Yes, but not mine." He sounded angry and continued, "Anyway, forget it."

"Ok. Sorry. So why did you invite me for coffee?" She looked straight into his eyes and smiled.

"I wanted to know you more. You are admirable and impressive," he replied, and couldn't stop smiling.

"Ah! You must be kidding, right?" She said.

"Actually, I am going to Australia to study. I have enrolled myself for a one-year course."

"What? Is that why you asked me for coffee?" She was shocked.

"Yes. Will you wait for me?"

"And what if I come to Australia?" she insisted.

He couldn't believe how committed she was and willing to go to any length for him.

He smiled and said, "I would love to know you more."

After finishing the coffee, Abeera thanked Samar for the invitation and left.

Abeera knew Samar was struggling inside. He wanted to do something of his own, and he had gotten angry at Abeera's question was the evidence. Abeera always thought these rich people had no reason to be unhappy, and money was the answer to everything. But what she experienced this time was completely the opposite. Even though Samar was good-looking, rich and well educated, he was still not happy.

Abeera was also looking for an escape, to move out from Pakistan. And now since Samar mentioned about Australia. She decided to move to Australia.

During the busiest days, Abeera's manager would ask her to stay late and work.

One day he tried to harass her, saying, "I can help you achieve your targets if you can give me something in return. And if you are ready, we can go to an evening party tonight and then to my apartment."

Abeera was disappointed with her manager's behavior. That night she stayed up, smoking and drinking and getting upset with herself for being a woman and asking God to help her. This incident reminded her of the last nasty episode.

In one of her previous jobs, she had resigned due to lack of courage. The manager was manipulative. He asked her to meet him outside the bank several times. And when Abeera continuously refused, he gave her a warning letter based on a silly mistake she made at work. Unable to handle this, she resigned.

Abeera became frustrated with the continuous manipulation and harassment at work.

Abeera's father had taught her to be independent but what he didn't teach her was how to protect herself from the dark side of men. Her father wasn't aware of her challenges at work. Though Abeera was friendly with her father, she never shared with him the horrible experiences she had with men at work.

But this time before her manager could give her a warning letter—she would become a victim once again—she went to him and submitted her resignation letter. Instead of facing it head on and fight for her respect, she was escaping from these men who made her life miserable.

Abeera had the same experience with some customers who wanted to meet her outside the bank. The same pattern, the same story, and the same behavior of men.

As an escape plan, she applied for further studies in Australia, assuming that when there are law and order in a country, it forces men to respect women and also she can continue to meet and know Samar more.

Abeera made her calculations. She only needed the enrolment and first semester fees and later she could work part-time, like other students in Australia, and survive. She spoke to her school friend who was living in Australia. She helped Abeera with all the details and also offered financial support to Abeera.

While Abeera was still serving the notice period. She got a call from one of her customers, whom she had met in a client meeting. He wanted Abeera to work for the company he worked for. He had been offering this job to Abeera for the last two years, but she showed no interest. He would call her time and time again, hoping she would change her mind and accept his offer.

This time he called with a new strategy. He offered to be friends, and she accepted. He invited her for dinner. They met at a restaurant. Once again, after dinner, he offered the job to her. He was determined and focused. Abeera was now looking for a job herself, so she accepted, but she didn't mention to him about her resignation and her plans of moving to Australia.

After finishing the notice period. Abeera joined the new company. For the first six months, she was on probation and only had to learn about the products, meet the clients, and assist her boss.

This gave her time to complete the formalities for her admission to the university in Australia. She prepared for her IELTS English language course, selected the university, and sorted out her finances.

Once Abeera cleared IELTS, she selected the university in Australia and decided that she will break the news with Samar. After Abeera shared the news of moving to Australia, Samar got delighted and told her, "Sorry I had been very busy with all the preparations, but I will definitely meet you more frequently in Australia and, as I said before, would love to know you more."

A few months passed. On New Year's Eve 2012.
Samar called her at a quarter to 12 midnight.
"Hi, hope you are well! I am at the airport and going to Australia. My phone

will work. Stay in touch and let me know when you reach Australia. We will catch up."

Abeera was delighted to hear from him. She spent the night enjoying with her friends. But she was imagining herself with Samar at the Opera House together on the next New Year's Eve.

Just a few days passed and a drama occurred at Abeera's place. Her brother-in-law (Sohail) had a big fight with Abeera's parents, asking them to stop her from going to Australia, after she had excitedly announced her plans.

Sohail didn't approve of her decision and told the family, "If she moves to Australia we will break ties with you all, and you will also have to vacate this house."

There was tension in Abeera's family.

In the past, Sohail and Abeera once worked in the same company. But he would often arrive late at work and was incompetent. Because of his consistent negligence at work, Sohail was asked to resign from the company. Sohail had a grudge in his heart that he had to resign because of Abeera. Even though Abeera had little to do with this. It was the management's decision. Sohail then borrowed money from his family to set up his business. Gradually, the business expanded, and he made loads of money. His greed for power, authority, and money had already destroyed his ties with his family.

Sohail owned the house Abeera and her family lived in. Although Abeera's brother Moiz made a few payments to pay off the house. But he could only pay 10 percent of the total amount. Abeera's parents feared to upset their son-in-law. So, instead, they requested Abeera to give up on studying abroad and asked her to visit Dubai and search for a job in Dubai.

At first Abeera got angry and told her parents, "It is my life, and I will do whatever I want to do. Sohail should mind his own business."

Abeera's parents lacked the courage to refuse their son-in-law.

Life was full of drama. Abeera couldn't find peace at home or at work.

Then, after a week.

Abeera agreed to her parents' request to visit Dubai. She took holidays from work and went to Dubai for two weeks. She dropped her resume to a few banks but didn't pursue a job seriously. Instead, she enjoyed Dubai's life and came back to Pakistan at the end of her holidays.

Back in Lahore, Abeera followed her routine life.

She told her parents, "I couldn't find a job in Dubai, but I have a well-paid job here. If the plan for Australia works, I will move, no matter what. And whatever decision I will take will be my choice not because of family pressures and interferences. Can you all stop treating me like a commodity, like a property? I am a human. Do I have no right over my life and my decisions?"

Abeera parents knew she would pursue her plans and it would be hard to convince her. They remained silent.

Abeera had faith that God had a plan for her and God will do that what is best for her.

After a month, she received a call from a bank in Dubai informing her that they had received her resume and that she should meet them at their main office in Lahore for an interview.

At first, she didn't care, but after a few days when she received the job offer letter, she had to take a decision.

They were offering her four times her current salary, a job in an international market and she will live with her brother, who she loved very much. But she had to give up on studying abroad and Samar.

Abeera changed her mind. She accepted the bank offer and decided to move to Dubai.

She shared the news with her manager at work, who discussed it with the Human Resources Manager of the company. The manager really liked Abeera. He tried to match the salary or provide Abeera more benefits with her present job. But Dubai, being a foreign market, was no comparison with Lahore and her current job. They couldn't meet the package that the bank in Dubai had offered her.

Everybody in the family was excited. Abeera did not envision that this job and relocation to Dubai will confront the realities of her loved ones.

She sent a message to Samar, "Sorry, I need to cancel my plan of coming to Australia. I have found a job in Dubai and I am moving there."

All he said was, "I am delighted for you. After I finish the course I will be back in Pakistan. If I am coming to Dubai, I will let you know."

Though she couldn't read his feelings from the message, in her mind she thought she still had a chance with him.

Inside Abeera was happy that she will be far from the criticisms, restrictions and pressures of her family. And especially the unnecessary interferences of Sohail.

After 2 months:

It all happened so quickly. She was very busy sorting her stuff, getting her dresses ready, shopping, and packing. She was not like other women who would shop 'till they dropped. She sensibly prepared a list of things she needed and the things she had to do, like selling her car, sorting her paperwork, organizing her wardrobe, and meeting her friends, her sisters and their in-laws.

July 2012

Soon it was time to say goodbye to Lahore.

The last time at the airport was special. It was a new beginning but also an ending.

Abeera moved to Dubai.

THE GIRL WHO LOVED HERSELF

Lessons we can learn from Abeera:

Taking the time out for self-mastery and reflecting is a step to self-love. Abeera realized: Beauty is not how you look; real beauty is how you feel inside yourself.

Abeera realized: Learning about yourself is one of the most important things in life.

Abeera learned to love herself. Love yourself like you love your loved ones. Love yourself like a baby. Hold yourself dear to you.

Often we think what we want is good for us, but only God knows what we need and what is best for us.

With the flow and the trust in God, you can reach where you are meant to be.

Chapter 3

The Solitude

DUBAI

Moiz and Abeera were very close since childhood. After Moiz moved to Dubai, Abeera would call him regularly. Whenever Moiz would come on holidays to Lahore, she would drop all her plans and dedicate all her time with him.

As Abeera arrived in Dubai, they decided to rent a two bedroom apartment.

Even if she had moved to Dubai, Abeera still wished things would work out between Samar and her. And so she continued talking to him.

However, Abeera still had many complex personal issues. Other than confusion, she was confrontational and defensive. At the earliest sign of betrayal and hurt she would hurt the other person, and because of this, she repeatedly broke the hearts of many men.

One day, like she confronted Daniyal, she confronted Samar too, "I know you are struggling with your life. Deep down you are not happy. I can't be waiting here for you forever. Your family business has a terrible reputation, and my father dislikes our friendship."

Samar felt dreadfully offended. He blocked Abeera from his life immediately and advised her never to communicate with him again.

2013

After six months in Dubai.

Most of Abeera's colleagues would party, drink and sleep with women.

In the beginning, she avoided these men but soon she became a part of their dirty habits. She allowed these men to enter her life and opened herself physically. She convinced herself that she was a free-spirited woman, and there was nothing wrong for having fun and to open herself physically to these kinds of men. Now she did not mourn over these men coming and leaving her life as she did not get emotionally attached to anyone. She called them, "No strings attached".

On the other side, some of her friends from Pakistan, those who wanted a serious relationship with Abeera visited her in Dubai. But for Abeera they were boring and had no adventure in their life, and what Abeera wanted was a life full of adventure.

But she was not going anywhere with these men. As the men she wanted a serious relationship with were the same men who only used her and never cared for her.

After a few months in Dubai.

Abeera got a loan from her bank of dirhams 500,000 on her father's request and paid Sohail for the house her parents lived in. Abeera's father had committed to Abeera that first, they would transfer the house in her mother's name and later her mother would sign the gift paper in Abeera's name. Abeera agreed.

Abeera went to Pakistan to see her family. After all the struggles and hardships of life now she could earn a handsome amount which she could spend on her family. She bought expensive gifts for her family and treated them for dinner.

On the last day of her visit to Lahore she dropped Samar a message, "Hey, hope you are good?" By this time Samar was already back in Lahore.
Samar replied in a few seconds, "Yes and you?" The message went through. It surprised Abeera.

"I'm all right. Have a flight to catch in one hour, going back to Dubai, just wanted to drop a hello."

"What! Why did you message me so late? I want to see you now," He said.

Abeera didn't want to miss seeing him. "Ok, sure! But I have little time."

"I am coming in ten minutes, don't worry."

Samar reached her door, picked her up, held her hand and confessed.

"I have always loved you, I have always adored you, I am exceptionally impressed with you, but we two are on different paths. You are settled, while I am still struggling. I have to achieve a lot in life. I am so sorry if I hurt you although I never intended to. I also wanted to apologize you for my rude behavior and clumsiness. Sorry. I hope you can forgive me."

They could barely meet for 15 minutes as Abeera had to rush to the airport and catch her flight. The airport was at least 30 minutes' drive away and her parents were waiting for her at home.

Samar impressed her, but he also confused her. She wondered if that meant there was hope for the relationship again. After another few hours, when she returned to Dubai, she tried to call Samar, but nothing had changed. He blocked her number again.

Abeera could not understand why he wanted to confess that he loved her and ended on a beautiful note. After all her experiences with men, she had not expected this. Samar gave her hope: hope to find someone humble, simple and down to earth.

Life is not always black and white. Sometimes grey areas make a life. Abeera thought.

Three years passed after Abeera's first breakup.

Her life had changed drastically. She was in Dubai and was enjoying a luxurious life.

However, her diaries were still full of poems, waiting to meet the man of her dreams.

I knew this day would come,
I knew my life was waiting for you

The gentleness of his touch,
The tenderness of his kiss

When we meet the universe dissolves,
A dance in the silence

My body dances in pleasure,
With you, the world is a beautiful place

The burning desire of the everlasting moments in your embrace
The moments of joy we share will remain sealed in my heart forever

I knew this day would come,
I knew my life was waiting for you

Abeera's weekends were often busy with her brother. They would shop for groceries, watch movies and visit their friends. Abeera's family would often visit them in Dubai. Abeera and Moiz would arrange tickets and pay for all their expense in Dubai.

This time Abeera's sister Savera also visited Dubai with her daughters.

Savera went to Moiz and told him, "You'd better be careful. Abeera will save all her money and ask you to spend your money. She is smart. You should stay vigilant."

Abeera overheard their conversation. Savera's jealousy had always surprised Abeera. Abeera was ambitious and her goals differed from her sister's. Her husband, Sohail, was also spending a lot of energy – and money – on becoming the new master in the family and, to do so, he was getting involved with everyone's life. He now tried to get Abeera's eldest sister divorced. He would always advise her to get divorced when she would share her petty issues with him. Savera knew all of this, and she was equally a part of her husband's dirty planning to get control of Abeera's family.

No matter what Savera and her husband, Sohail would do, it changed nothing in Abeera's relation with her father and her brother. Abeera's brother had always admired Abeera for her support and care. And they were proud of how successful Abeera had now become. Since childhood, Abeera loved her brother and her father above everyone.

Despite the confusion in her mind and heart, Abeera was still hoping someone she got attracted to would someday commit to her.

Abeera had not forgotten Samar yet but she could do nothing.

Samar had cut off ties with her. And so her attention turned elsewhere.

Abeera had a friend, Kamal who was living in Dubai. They had studied at the same university and had known each other for the last four years. Abeera felt attracted to him. She found dominant, aggressive men more appealing because of the protection they could offer.

She was aggressive and dominating too because of her lack of self-love, her fear of loss and her fear of looking weak. Instead of understanding the reasons for her attraction towards these kinds of men, she thought it was love.

So she proposed marriage to Kamal. Deep down, she thought *I'm not hiding my feelings.* She convinced herself that Kamal had every reason to marry her. And she proposed Kamal in an email.

From: Abeera Shaikh
Date: April 13, 2013 10:00
Subject: Proposal
To: Kamal

Hello Kamal,

Hope you are well!

This might come as a surprise, but something about you has attracted me to you since the first day I saw you. Having no courage to tell you in person, I preferred writing to you.

I have thought about the two of us, and, at least from my side, you are the first man I have the courage to propose marriage to. I don't know if this is love.

I know you are one year younger than me and still studying, but that is not important. I will support you always with your studies and career, I promise.

I have recently moved to Dubai and feel very lucky that you are here too.

I know you are planning to take over your father's business after you finish your studies. I can quit my work and join your company. We both can work together. That will be perfect for our future.

Good luck in your studies. I will wait eagerly for your reply.

Yours ever loving,

Abeera

Abeera was excitedly waiting for Kamal's reply and had already built a future with him in her mind.

Two days passed.

She didn't hear from him. She got worried and went to Amir to get his opinion on why Kamal had not responded yet.

Amir became upset with her and told her, "This is not the way to propose to a man. You are a woman. You should not do the job of a man. And email – is that a business proposal or what? This email is like a professional letter. At least you could have written only about your love for him rather than your interest in joining his business and your future with him. It looks like a deal, and this is not how love is. Love is not a business, love is not a deal. Love is pure. In love, the heart speaks, not the mind."

This surprised Abeera. She asked, "Why, what is so wrong?"

He explained to her again, "You are again putting yourself at someone else's disposal, and even after your breakup, you haven't learned to respect yourself enough. You are too direct, planned and calculated in your email. I am sure this email will hurt Kamal's ego. And besides, if he really loved you, by now you would have known it. And, sorry, no matter how open-minded and free-spirited you think you are, you also need to understand what works with men."

Abeera became so confused and had nothing to say. She without saying a word left.

Another day passed.

She didn't hear from Kamal. She called him and inquired, in her dominating style, "Why haven't you responded to my email?"

He replied in a soft tone, "I am sorry, I am not interested in marrying anyone: not you, nor any other woman. I thought it would offend you. That is why I didn't reply."

She responded angrily, "But at least have the courtesy to reply. It is a goddamn proposal. There is nothing wrong in that!" And she hung up.

Abeera smoked all night, and once again felt heartbroken. She realized that she should understand that the silence of a man can sometimes mean he is not interested in what you have offered, or maybe he is interested in something else and does not want to let his chance go.

A few days later.
Kamal called her and invited her to a coffee shop. Abeera got excited that maybe he had changed his mind and was now ready for a relationship with her.
She went to see him at the coffee shop but after they finished the coffee. Kamal told her, "I am only interested in sleeping with you."
This was the last thing she had expected from the man she had proposed marriage to. How could a man be so inconsiderate about his selfish desires? He does not even respect a woman who wanted to commit to him.
She wondered, *if all a man wants is a woman with two legs. Does sincerity even matter? Is every woman going through the same horrible experiences I do? Why are we women created? For what? To see men harassing us, and to make our lives miserable?*
She became so upset with all these experiences. She decided she will never commit to anyone and continued passing her time with men who were bad boys, alcoholics and flirts.

August 2013
After Kamal, Khan, one of her friends living in Australia, proposed to Abeera for marriage.
Khan lived in Australia. Abeera and Khan met once in Dubai a few weeks ago as Khan was traveling from Dubai to Punjab (In Pakistan) to see his relatives.
Abeera was confused about Khan. She did not feel very attractive to him but at the same time, she was so desperate to get married that she did not want to miss the opportunity to finally get married.
She shared Khan's proposal with her father, and he advised her, "You can have a contract marriage of two years, he should gift you a property for your security. The second condition is that he should settle in Dubai with you rather than you leaving Dubai and your job. The third condition, in the interim you will have no child till you take a decision to move in with him. If he agrees to all these conditions, you can marry him. As our religion does not permit a 'live in relationship' before marriage so we have to take a wise decision."
Abeera became upset with these ideas of her father, "Contract marriage," meaning marriage of convenience. *All my life my father had taught me that "marriages are made in Heaven." Then what happened today? What kind of a faith is this? If one believes truly that marriage is a relationship made by God then*

does it matter whether the relationship stays forever or not? We can't ridicule our faith like this.

Abeera felt Khan will not agree to all these conditions. She did not tell anything to Khan and refuse the proposal.

Though inside Abeera was very disappointed with her dream of marriage being shattered again and again.

After a while of having fun and no serious relationship, she became exhausted with partying and sick and tired of herself.

One day she confronted herself: *What the hell are you doing and what the hell do you want from life? You came to Dubai to save yourself from the manipulation and harassment of men but look what you have done to yourself. Partying, drinking, and one man after the other. Is that it? Is that what you wanted to do with your freedom? Can you even think beyond that? Where are you headed to? What do you want from life?*

The next day she googled, "How to get peace?" She came across a few websites for meditation. One of them was the web page of a Sufi school. She emailed the address provided and inquired about meditation. Some guy named Imran responded to her email and invited her to try the meditation on the coming Thursday.

A few days passed.

But the questions kept coming. Where were they coming from, suddenly? The charm of the new city had worn off now. The charm of a new place, a new relationship, a new job didn't stay with her for long. *But what is it that stays with you forever? Is 'happiness forever?' something that ever existed? Where do I get the formula for true happiness?* That was it. She desperately wanted something new.

It was Thursday now. Abeera and her friend, Saima went to Al Barsha for meditation. They took one hour to reach the address provided. It was at the opposite end of Dubai to where she and Saima lived.

They went inside. There was a beautiful couple, a very attractive, well-groomed, blonde young woman with long silky hair, and a man who was short but elegantly dressed and very handsome. He had a lovely British accent. Were they British? He didn't have a Western name though. They looked super wealthy, with a huge villa, a big garden, a big pool and a few fancy cars in the parking lot.

After a little introduction, the man explained to them, "Mediation is a tool to disconnect from everything and connect with God. Sufi meditation is the closest translation for the Arabic word 'Muraqaba'. It is directed towards the heart since the heart is the center and the seat of love and divine inspiration. Sufi Meditation has levels and stages. One needs a guide to take the steps of meditation. The potentiality, desires, demands, and attractions of a seeker will determine the teacher he or she will find along the way. Your guide will take you to a spiritual and divine destination but for that you may need to undertake purification, to purify yourself." Right after that, he added, "Now we will switch off the lights, close our eyes, and say the intention towards the heart meditation, and sit in the dark for 45 minutes."

Abeera and Saima looked at each other, puzzled.

They then switched the lights off.

Abeera was terrified. *What kind of meditation is this? This is frightening. I want to find true happiness and satisfaction but by sitting in this dark, this is impossible! Have I lost my mind or what? And who knows–they might invite people here to murder. There are all kinds of crimes happening on this Earth. How can I fall into this trap? How can I be a fool? I should stand up, get over this and go back before I am killed and they send my dead body to Pakistan!*

The 45 minutes were not less than a near death experience. All kinds of fears haunted Abeera. She could barely close her eyes, and, after every few minutes, she would open her eyes and look around, but it was so dark she couldn't see anything. All she could do was pray that she gets back home without getting into any trouble.

Finally, the 45 minutes were over, everybody was alive, they switched the lights on, and they both breathed in peace.

Abeera and Saima weren't sure if they would ever want to attend any more meditation sessions. They thanked the couple for the invitation and left.

On the way back, Abeera and Saima shared their experiences with each other. They laughed their heads off at how terrified they felt.

Finally, Abeera was exhausted from trying her luck again and again with men, so now she would either see Saima or stay with her brother when he was home. Otherwise, she would spend the evening alone at home, or, other times, stay late at work.

A few days staying at home and doing nothing was an indescribable experience for her.

She really enjoyed it.

But she was still alone, and alone she would write a poem or two to express her sadness, express her feelings of loneliness, and listen to old rhyming couplets. Abeera realized that something bigger was missing. If money, freedom and security are all that one wanted in life. It should satisfy her. But despite having all this she was still unhappy and dissatisfied with her life. Her handbag was full of papers, sometimes even blank papers. She would write at coffee shops or while waiting for regular meetings. That would bring out something she wasn't aware of, often not knowing where it came from, but it had honesty and purity in its message.

Once she wrote, "Writing helps us acknowledge what we have within ourselves. Even when there are moments you feel out of peace, you can get your peace back when you connect with yourself."

November 2013

Abeera enjoyed being with herself so much that she travelled to Singapore alone.

She went to the airport, checked in, and had her usual coffee with a croissant while waiting for boarding. After the flight boarded, she watched a movie and read a book on the flight.

All this time was only for herself: no phone calls, no friends, and no familiar people around, a world for herself, with no validation and without the burden of work the next day or the pressure of her own goals in her mind. She felt free.

After reaching Singapore Airport, the driver from the hotel picked her up, and she checked into the hotel. The hotel was not too good. She realized that when traveling next time; she needed to check the details of the hotel rather than relying on the travel agent.

She dropped her luggage, got freshened up and went out onto the streets of Singapore. It was very refreshing.

She walked a few meters and met a lady from South Africa sitting on a bench writing a letter. She initiated a conversation with her. The lady showed Abeera the letters she was writing for her family. It surprised Abeera—people in this century full of technology still prefer writing letters. Somehow she got motivated about her writing skills. There are still people who prefer writing letters. In the past, she had written many thank-you notes and poems in love for her father and her brother.

In the next few minutes, she met a Filipino girl. They became friends. *This place was brilliant and people are so friendly,* she thought. The girl introduced Abeera immediately to her friends. The night became so amazing, meeting different people from different countries.

Then, in the middle of the night, she sat for a while on a bench and wondered, *why is it called madness to enjoy your own company and spend time in solitude? Only through solitude can I know my state, my inner state of being. My outer state affects my inner state. If my inner state is fine, everything outside me will be fine. That inner self is the center of my existence and my life.*

The next day.

The tour guide arrived right on time. The journey for the city tour began. There were many people from different religions on the tour. Abeera became friends with them, drank the same water and ate from the same plate.

Abeera also became friends with Farhan on the tour bus. Their main discussions were about Eastern societies and their challenges. Even though the discussions were not intimate, Abeera felt Farhan wanted to tell her something. A few times she thought he said something, and she asked him, "Did you speak to me?" he replied, "Nothing."

The quest started when she entered the Buddhist temple. Idol worshiping had always bothered her. What can an idol do? An idol can't protect itself. How can it provide, protect and take care of others? But maybe it is with faith; everybody has their own faith. They need to decide for themselves. *Our faiths are different, but, I have no right to be judgemental or even think I am right or they are wrong or anybody is inferior or superior. Perhaps that's what my religion, Islam teaches me, to respect everyone and their religions.*

Abeera thought, *Humanity first: all religions are same at the core. No religion promotes hatred, wars, crime, cheating, fraud, etc. At the core of all religions is love, harmony, compassion, and peace; and we are all humans, having different experiences, different backgrounds, different cultures, different perceptions and perhaps different mind-sets.*

She realized that the essence of every human being is same; the problem is only in the mindset, the rigidness of her beliefs and her thoughts. If she could do herself a favor and let go of her personal opinions of people and situations, she would enjoy every bit of her trip. And that is what she did, and that made her trip fantastic.

For the first time, she realized the pleasure of being with herself, with her own bunch of experiences. The pressures of the family were fine and they don't have to be with her all the time.

It was immensely beautiful to see the infinity pool that gave her its own freshness that made her feel alive in every fibre of her being. The view from the top was amazing, the beauty was intoxicating, and she felt completely mesmerized.

The tour guides, the receptionists, the taxi drivers – all were cooperative.

There was a German guy from Abu Dhabi who told her to join his group and be friends with them. She refused him and enjoyed on her own. She could see her strong sense of self in the form of her independence, yet fully controlled and satisfied.

In life, we often have the choice to decide. She was glad to know what to refuse and what to accept.

She realized that human beings are God's greatest creation, but we rarely acknowledge that and get lost in the quests of our own minds and mundane lives, running after our desire for money, love and relationships, without accepting how life unfolds itself in any moment.

The trip ended, and it delighted her.

Abeera was now coming back to Dubai with her learned lessons in Singapore.

Lessons we can learn from Abeera:

Abeera realized: The roles you play in your life, at your office, with your bosses, with your colleagues and with the world are not who you are. Who you are is far beyond all the turbulence you have in your mind-made image of yourself and your accumulated experiences.

Abeera realized: Things can never be better than what they are right at this moment. The flower blossoms at its own pace. The earth revolves in its own way; it couldn't be otherwise. Nature is silent and at peace. There is a reason you are where you are. Worrying is just creating problems, a never-ending series.

Abeera realized: When you are at peace with yourself, you don't need a company or people to remind you of your worth. You are already a whole, with everything inside your own self.

Nothing can be more fascinating than being with one's self completely. Abeera realized: The real adventure of life is only when we step out of our own comfort zone, take things as opportunities and let the flow of life take its own course.

Perhaps freedom also gives you the opportunity to make wise choices.

Abeera realized: Running after desires and mundane stuff does not give us peace. Peace is within us and contentment is within us.

Abeera realized: Love is between you and you. If you keep looking for love outside you. You will always remain disappointed.

Abeera realized: Happiness does not come from money, materials or possessions. Happiness comes from within oneself.

Chapter 4

The Hurt in Relationships

December 2013

It was Moiz's wedding.

A few months before, Moiz's friend recommended a girl for Moiz to get married to. Things progressed quickly and after a short while, Moiz requested the family to visit them for the wedding proposal. Both the families agreed upon the marriage after the first visit.

The wedding took place in Lahore and comprised many functions. Late night singing ceremonies and many other rituals took place throughout the day. Everyone was very excited. They welcomed guests from Karachi and Islamabad.

Abeera gifted expensive gold necklace and gold bangles to Moiz's wife on their wedding. Abeera also bought expensive gifts for her family; a home theatre system for her father, a mobile phone for her brother, gold bangles for her mother, and designer clothes for Savera's daughters.

Abeera stayed for a few days with the family and then travelled back to Dubai. Moiz stayed in Lahore to celebrate the New Year Eve and a few days of January with his wife and came back to Dubai after a few days with his wife.

It was just a week they arrived in Dubai and everything changed in Abeera's life. The brother she had a lovely relationship was now fighting with Abeera every day. And it was the same story: his wife always misunderstood Abeera and complained to Moiz and he would fight with Abeera.

The situation got worse and worse. And one day, Moiz told Abeera, "Why don't you go away and leave this apartment?"

Abeera was deeply offended. Not only she shared the rent of the apartment with Moiz but Abeera specifically addressed that question at the time of the marriage and had asked the family and Moiz if she could move out after Moiz's marriage. But they had refused.

However, confidently Abeera replied, "Let me ask dad to come to Dubai and sort this out. I don't want to stay here too. Mom, dad and you had asked me earlier to stay with you. Otherwise, I would have left by now. And don't talk to me like this. I equally share the rent with you. It is not just your apartment. It's mine too."

Abeera called her father and explained what had been happening. To which he angrily replied, "Don't worry, he can't do this to you. I will sort it. Send me the ticket I will come to Dubai." Abeera sent the tickets to him.

In a week's time, their father reached Dubai.

January 2014

Abeera picked up her father from the airport.

The Hurt in Relationships

The next day was a day filled with sorrow and pain. Abeera didn't know that God tests the faith of his believer. After she woke up in the morning to get ready for work, her dad commanded, "I have concluded. Either you compromise with your brother and his wife, or just leave." After a pause, he continued, "You are familiar with Dubai now!"

It shocked Abeera. The ground seemed to slip away beneath her feet at that moment.

Somehow, I had thought my father understood me more than anyone else, but there it was. (In Eastern Societies, parents do not ask daughters to leave their family's house. It is a culture that they stay with their parents until they get married. After marriage, they move to their husband's home; either with his joint family or separately with the husband.)

"Dad, what did you say?" She shockingly replied.

He repeated what he had said, "I meant you can live alone. You are independent, -- and you are capable now."

"Dad, are you serious?" Abeera's voice shivering, as if she had lost her senses.

"Yes, that's what I said."

Abeera did not know what to say and remained silent thinking, *was it true that he had asked me to leave? Who asks his daughter to leave? These days, children ask their parents to leave when they are old. But he had asked me to leave.*

"All right, I will tell Mom what you said," Abeera angrily replied.

Her father responded, "What can your mom do? Go tell whoever you want to."

Abeera got ready and left for work. After she reached work. With tears rolling down her cheeks, she called her mother.

"Mom, you know what Dad said?"

"Stop crying. Go ahead," she replied hastily.

"Mom, he asked me to compromise or leave!"

"What did he say?" Abeera's mother couldn't believe it either like Abeera.

"Yes, Mom. He said I should leave. He knows I will never compromise on my self-respect."

"Why should you leave and why should you compromise?" she angrily replied, "But what can I say? I don't understand your dad," she added.

The bank doors were about to open.

"I need to put the phone down now. I'll talk to you later. Bye, Mom."

Abeera's mother called her after an hour and told her, "I'm sorry, but I can't help. Your father wants you to leave. You can go home, take your clothes and find a place to stay."

"But mom — where will I stay?" Abeera's voice shivering.

Her mom replied, "I am Sorry. I don't know."

Soon it was night and Abeera had finished from work. Abeera had no courage to enter the same place from where she had been asked to leave.

I wish I was dead before facing this embarrassment today. Abeera told herself.

When Abeera reached home, no one was there. She took a small bag, some of her clothes, shoes and left.

Abeera didn't have many friends in Dubai. Abeera called Saima and asked her, "If she could stay with them for a few days?"

Saima was living with her mother. They were from Pakistan but they were living in Dubai because of Saima's education.

Saima replied, "You are more than welcome." In fact, she was very excited that Abeera was coming to stay with them.

After Abeera reached Saima's place, it was late, she had dinner and went to a room, where she could sleep.

Abeera felt terribly hurt and couldn't sleep that night. She prayed, *God, please give me courage. I feel weak. I have never felt so weak, so many emotions crossing over, so many thoughts. Was I actually a burden on anyone? My brother and I shared the rent. For years I have been working and paid for my studies myself. I paid for the house for my parents. I did all I could, only to see this today? Dad used to say I was his favorite daughter. He would say I had asked nothing from them. Then how could he be so inconsiderate to his daughter today?*

The next day, Ameen called Abeera. She felt so powerless, incapable, and inferior.

Abeera's mother and Ameen called Abeera's father a few times, but he didn't talk to anyone in detail and told them, "I have already given my decision and I don't want to talk on this subject with anyone."

The week passed and Abeera was crying in pain, asking for God's help.

Abeera shared the story with Saima, "Truth is so relentless. I don't wonder why people avoid it. All my life I knew I was a commodity being used, and now when it's on the surface, I hate it."

Saima replied, "Abeera, Didn't you understand your dad? What do you expect? His sincere concern? You gave him what he wanted. And you expected that he would reciprocate your love. But he didn't. He is what he is. You expected something, and now you are feeling bad about it."

Abeera was bogged down, "I didn't think to get his love and attention. He always loved me. Then what happened today? What has changed? He was always supportive. He used to say I was his best daughter. How can he throw the best daughter out?"

Saima's mother was listening to them quietly. She intervened, "I understand. It is a shock to you. Parents don't ask children to leave. Especially a daughter in the East. In the West maybe. But don't worry you can stay as long as you want to, and everything will be fine. God will sort everything for you. I will pray for you. You should talk to your father about it again."

Abeera was *quiet. Is it true? I can't believe it. My expectations of being loved reciprocally from 'My father?' Is it even true we are talking about a father and a daughter relationship? I thought God can't be everywhere that is why He sent our parents. And here I am? Some words are so painful I can't even repeat them to myself. How do I ask him again? And ask what – to insult me once again?*

Abeera had a few discussions with Saima's mother and she became friendly with her too. Saima's mother was a simple, wise and also a very spiritual woman.

After ten days.

Sohail arrived in Dubai for a business meeting. He invited the family for dinner, called Abeera and told her, "I will sort it out, don't worry." Sohail had full control of Abeera's father. Her father was discussing everything with Sohail rather than his own daughter.

They all met at the restaurant. This was the first time in Abeera's life there was silence between Abeera and her father. She felt suffocated. The man she was sitting with had become an ordinary man for her, a man she no longer trusted. What could they possibly discuss? Her father had decided already. He had always been dominating and controlling. And what difference would a discussion make now? Could he take his words back? Would she get the same love and respect she got from him once? Would the relationship go back to how it was before? They always had various discussions and took several decisions together, but today her father had left her alone.

Sohail, Abeera, and her father met for coffee after dinner in Sohail's hotel room. Sohail confronted Abeera's father for his decision who replied, "That was the best fix."

"What? To ask your daughter to leave is a fix?" Abeera got angry at her father. She stood up the chair.

Sohail asked Abeera to wait downstairs in the lobby until he finishes his discussion with her father alone.

After 30 minutes of discussion, Sohail called Abeera and asked her to come to his room.

Abeera's father apologized to her and they decided that Abeera would come back home.

Inside Abeera felt unworthy and powerless. Her brother-in-law was more important, her sister-in-law was more important, and her father's now favorite was everyone but her. Abeera stood as no one before her father. Abeera had never predicted that things could change in just a matter of few days.

The next day Abeera came back home.

For another few nights, Abeera's father would go into Moiz's room and they would have dinner together. Nobody asked Abeera if she had had dinner or not.

She would sleep with an empty stomach.

Nobody was talking to Abeera even when she came back home. It felt as if she was a stranger in her own place.

Two weeks later,

Abeera's father went back to Lahore.

Although Abeera's father was still not talking to her, she still took time out from her work and met her father at the airport. He didn't talk to her. He was behaving strangely. It was as if it was Abeera who had kicked him out.

Abeera didn't know what to say, she stood quietly and thought, *Just because he is my father, it doesn't give him the right to hurt and insult me. I love him but not more than myself, nor do I allow anyone to disrespect me, even if it is my dad. Why is he doing the emotional drama now, and for what? What does he expect from me? To still shower my love on him? This is ridiculous. I can't stand the hypocrisy of people, and unfortunately, on the other side is my father.*

Abeera's father went back to Pakistan. Abeera was still living with her brother and his wife. But inside she felt depressed and wanted an escape for the weekend and relax.

March 2014

Abeera searched for a travel deal to book for the weekend. Nepal looked the most convenient place. She didn't have to wait for a visa. Before booking the deal, she emailed the agent who responded immediately, even though it was late in Nepal and the offices were closed.

Maybe certain things are meant to happen, and when they do, everything becomes easy.

She booked the travel deal and the tickets. On the way, back home. Abeera called her brother and informed him she would travel that night. He said 'ok' and put the phone down.

The next minute, Abeera's mom called her from Pakistan and inquired, "Where are you going, and why alone?"

"Mom, I am not traveling alone for the first time. Don't worry. After the way your husband and son had been treating me, I can't believe you can even question me like this. Anyway, I want to spend time alone."

Her mother replied, "Your father is apologetic. Everything is fine now. You should forgive him. We are humans. We are not perfect, and we make mistakes."

"Apologetic? Mistake? Forgiveness? What do you mean mom? You do not know how he treated me when I came back home. In reality, dad is not apologetic. His apology was just a word, a mere formality. I wonder what game he is playing with me. Mom, please, just leave me alone. I don't want to talk about anything."

"Ok, fine. Do what you want to." Abeera's mother hung up.

Abeera had never imagined Moiz would become so selfish and inconsiderate after his marriage. Even when her brother in laws were trying to help her, Moiz offered no help.

Moiz rather felt happy that dad had asked her to leave.

Abeera was flying early in the morning from Sharjah airport. She booked a cab and headed to the airport. Abeera didn't want to think about anything except enjoying her trip. She checked in. It was a four-hour flight.

The time passed quickly. She watched a few movies and read a book.

The tour guide from the hotel arrived at the Kathmandu Airport to pick her up and dropped her at the hotel.

She spent a while in the hotel, said prayers, and got dressed up in a nice attire to deviate her mind from her sorrows and enjoy the city tour with the travel guide.

They travelled around the city. The weather was lovely. But when you are unhappy inside, the weather makes no difference to you.

After a day tour. In the evening, they had coffee and some snacks in a restaurant. Then the tour guide dropped Abeera back to the hotel. The hotel was fine, but it was the least of her concerns.

Abeera walked in the room for a while and thought, when people die, you feel sorrowful. But what do you do when relationships die, even when people are alive? Even though I am still living with my brother, the relationship has died. Human love is full of emotional turmoil. Can I ever get peace amid all this?

THE GIRL WHO LOVED HERSELF

Abeera wanted to go to the bar downstairs and drink, but she had no courage. She was not in her right mind. She was so heartbroken, and she knew drinking might aggravate the pain. Who knew where she might end up tomorrow?

She stayed in her room, witnessing the energy imbalances within her: the sensations, the vibrations in her body because of the pressure she had on herself.

All she had was a pen, some papers, and the book she was reading. She picked up the pen and wrote, *"I am in pain. I want to die."*

And then the inner talk.

> *All your life you have been running away from reality when it becomes tough. When you broke up with your ex-boyfriend you gave into your dirty habits. When you couldn't handle the harassment of people, you wanted to escape to Australia. And now, when you can't handle the reality of your relationships, you want to die. When reality is painful all you want to do is die.*
>
> *Yes, a graveyard is peaceful, I suppose.*
>
> *You learned inner peace is a matter of acceptance. But you still want to escape from the reality when life becomes tough.*
>
> *But the reality is so harsh, so brutal, and so unfair. How do I get the courage to accept it?*
>
> *Life is unpredictable and challenging. It pushes you to the limits, brings discomfort. But that's what life is, a journey. Remember when you had a breakup, how miserable you felt? But soon everything returned to normal. In fact, it was a turning point in your life. These experiences are a blessing. They help you learn and grow. Did you not learn that?*
>
> *I did. But how do I find a way to acceptance in this painful journey? I don't want to even think about the future. I have lost all hopes and expectations from everything and everyone in life. It is 4 am. I could not sleep. I feel exhausted. Many days have passed since I felt loved, cared, and protected. What my dad said is still on my mind and I can't stop thinking about it.*

Finally, Abeera could sleep. But only for two hours.

The next morning the tour guide picked her up again. The day was again filled with beautiful scenery, mountains and forests. They visited many temples and Abeera prayed at all the temples, "God, You have control over everything, and only You know what will give peace to my heart."

After spending all day traveling and sightseeing, they reached Nagarkot.

Nagarkot is a village, 32km from Kathmandu, packed with hotels, having one of the broadest views of the Himalaya, with eight ranges visible. By the time they reached Nagarkot, it was already dark and time for dinner.

Abeera had dinner at the restaurant in the hotel and headed to her room.

The weather was cloudy and foggy. *How romantic would it be if I had someone with me? The lovely weather, the fire, me and him?* Abeera laughed at herself, *you and your wishes!*

Abeera spent a few hours in the room reading a book and watching a movie on the television. But again she couldn't sleep.

At midnight the electricity went out. Abeera waited for a while for the electricity to come back but when it didn't she headed to the reception using the torch of her mobile.

She found nobody at the reception. A guard was sitting outside the hotel. She went to him and inquired, "When will the electricity come back on?"

He replied, "It might take a few hours, madam, but I can't say."

"And why did you not switch on the generator?" She confidently asked.

"Madam, we don't have a generator," he responded politely.

"What? And how do you expect people to stay in the dark?"

"Madam, I don't know, but we never had a generator." He looked irritated. Maybe no one had never asked him this question before.

Abeera went back to the room. She wanted to escape from her sadness but here she was miserable again. Her phone had only 30 percent charge left.

Luckily, there was a small candle she could light in the room.

Abeera picked up a paper and wrote:

What brings me here? I don't know. My phone does not work on roaming. I can't call anyone. Is it true that when you need someone or something, no one and nothing is there for you? I am all alone here with my money, cards, diamond rings, and an expensive watch. What should I do? How do I escape from this dark night?

In childhood, I always enjoyed the silence of the night, but today this dark, gloomy, dusky, and silent night is frightening. Sometimes I wish life had a fast-forward button. I would fast-forward many occasions in life. But in life, you can't remove this moment and jump from here to there without experiencing this

THE GIRL WHO LOVED HERSELF

moment, no matter how challenging or intolerably painful it becomes.

Just next to Abeera's room was a Japanese girl with some people. Abeera could hear them talking, laughing, singing, enjoying and maybe even drinking.

At first, Abeera wanted to knock on their door and join them, but deep inside it scared her. Abeera thought to wait at the reception until the electricity came back on. But how could she trust a guard? Many horror movies were crossing her mind. It also reminded her of the movies she had watched, how men can get women into trouble. Now she became even more terrified.

The room had a balcony. She thought of opening the balcony door but needed the courage to do so. She had none left. The darkness around scared her too.

After considering all plans of escape, finally, she realized there was nothing she wanted to do. She should better stay in the room and be completely with herself. She was constantly explaining to herself that all these fears were in her head.

A few hours with no electricity, in a place too far away, no phone, no internet. Even the people in the next room had slept as she couldn't hear them anymore. It was silent.

Abeera picked up a paper again and wrote:

"God knows everything.
If He takes away something, He will give you something better.
Perhaps God is the biggest Compensator.
If someone is plotting against you, God is plotting something against them.
God is the biggest Plotter.
Don't curse the pain and agony you are going through. God is the biggest Healer.
Don't worry about the darkness around. God is the biggest Protector.
God has a plan for you. Perhaps God is the biggest Planner.
Nobody can steal what God has destined for you. God is the biggest Provider."

Abeera couldnot stop thinking,

Miraculous! What did I write? What does this mean? Where is it coming from? Is this why my soul brought me here? To hear God, you need to go away from everything, in the dark, in the mountains and give up on the most important relationships in your life. Is it true?

The Hurt in Relationships

Is it God talking to me on this paper? This is unbelievable. I searched for God in relationships. I searched for God in the clouds. I searched for God in many men who I thought might be my man of dreams. I thought God can't be everywhere that is why He made my parents. But every time, I failed. I could not find God.
(In the East some people believe husbands are God-like and some people believe parents are God-like. Abeera was taught this since childhood.)

If God is found in my parents, my father would never hurt me, would he? If God is found in my man of dreams, my struggles wouldn't hurt me so much, would they? If God is found in the clouds, I would have seen Him long ago when I was young.

Abeera's family never understood why she would sit on the terrace for hours.

In the process of searching God, her parents told her that God is separate from us. And she might never see Him.

But was it God talking to her on this paper? Abeera couldn't stop thinkin*g: Is there a plan for me? Do I need to give up on everything to find God? Am I here to learn this?*

Abeera picked up the pen and wrote again:

*"If I ever return alive from this place,
I must believe God knows everything. He is the greatest Healer, Plotter, Planner, Provider, Protector, and Compensator.
If He wants me to stay alive and go back to Dubai, I am here only to learn the lessons. I must always remember that I need nobody but God.
I must leave everything to Him and trust Him. He has a plan for me.
Am I here to learn this lesson? Is this what my soul was telling me that I couldn't have learned otherwise?"*

Abeera's heart wept again. She had loved her father so much, her brother so much. *How could my dad ever do this? Does he not need me anymore? Is it all about needing a daughter? Was there anything missing in my love? Have I not made him proud of me?*

So many questions were on Abeera's mind; some questions remain unanswered. No matter how much you question, it won't change the reality of the relationship.

THE GIRL WHO LOVED HERSELF

She keeps re-reading what she wrote:

*"If I ever return alive from this place,
I must believe God knows everything. He is the greatest Healer, Plotter, Planner, Provider, Protector, and Compensator.
If He wants me to stay alive and go back to Dubai, I am here only to learn the lessons. I must always remember that I need nobody but God. I must leave everything to Him and trust Him. He has a plan for me.
Am I here to learn this lesson? Is this what my soul was telling me that I couldn't have learned otherwise?"*

Where has life brought me? Everything is an illusion, every relationship is an illusion, things change, people change and life never remains the same. Abeera thought.

The electricity came back. She didn't die, no ghost came, nobody climbed from the balcony, and nobody broke down the door. *I am alive. Yes, I am alive.* She puts on the television and slept in a little while. After so many days she could have a proper sleep. The receptionist called her early in the morning to see the sunrise, but she didn't wake up. Perhaps the sunrise, the mountains, the beautiful weather are for people who are happy. What good can these things do to a person who is heartbroken?

In the morning Abeera woke up and went to the hotel lobby for breakfast. There were several people in the lobby. Some tourist groups and some families. Abeera looked at them in surprise, wondering: *Do these families also hurt their loved ones?*

Then she saw a girl holding a guy's hand, *oh, that looks so romantic. Is she certain this guy will always love her and never hurt her? Or has God written this misfortune only in my life?*

Now she had to travel back to Kathmandu. Kathmandu is a lively city. She didn't need to worry about the dark night again.

Abeera listened to some old music while traveling back to Kathmandu.

Abeera reached the hotel; it looked better. Her phone was still not working on roaming but she could connect to WIFI. Her colleague sent her a message on social media. "Your manager was looking for you."

"But why?" she replied, "I had the weekend off."

Abeera didn't care as she was traveling back to Dubai the next day. And besides, she needed to pull herself together to face the different faces and realities of her relationships.

The next day she took the flight back to UAE. The last episode in her family still hurt her.

Her state remained unchanged, but acceptance became easier. She was still bombarded with ample questions, having no answers.

She reached UAE, with her soul's lesson, took a cab, and in 20 minutes she reached home.

But she had no words to express her anguish, only sad poetry and songs of sorrows, resonated with her. Abeera wondered, *do all lovers have to go through this pain? Who are these people who write and sing sad lyrics and poetry? Do they go through the same sadness? Are happiness and sadness the two sides of the same story? People who you love, hurt you more. Is this a rule?*

After ten minutes the doorbell rang. Abeera opened the door. It was the Human Resource Manager and the bank officer.

"Hey, you are here! We heard you were missing."

"What?" Abeera gave a weird smile, "Who said that?"

"Your manager wrote an email to the General Manager saying you were missing."

"Did he? I didn't suspect," Abeera replied.

The Human Resources Manager said, "Yes, I told him it's just a matter of one day and Abeera might be sick. But you know the way he goes on. Even the General Manager got worried."

"But you had my brother's number in my profile. You could have contacted him. Anyway, no worries. I will call the General Manager now," Abeera replied with confidence.

She dialled the number of the General Manager from her phone, "Hello, Sir. Abeera here. I apologize for the misunderstanding. It was my Saturday off, and I was traveling. I booked my flights at the last minute. That is why I couldn't inform my manager."

Abeera thought, *nothing gives you more power than honesty, no matter what may happen. One should be honest. I know that God is the greatest, and He knows about everything. Who do I need to lie to and for what? What more can I lose? The loves of my life, my father and my brother don't care. My sisters never bothered calling me. If this is where I stand today, then I am not scared of losing anything. I have nothing more to lose.*

The General Manager replied, "This is negligence and carelessness. You should have informed the bank about your travel. Regardless."

"Yes, sir. My phone wasn't working on roaming, otherwise, I would have definitely called."

"That is not acceptable. See you at work." He hung up.

Abeera went to the bank. She meets the manager, "Sir, don't worry. I am here, alive and well."

He explained that he became worried about her. Without listening to anything, Abeera left his room.

He emailed her asking for a written explanation.

Before she could respond, Abeera got a call from Amir, who had recently moved to Dubai and wanted to surprise her, "When did you arrive? I have been calling you, I wanted to surprise you."

Abeera was delighted that Amir had moved to Dubai. Although she was sharing things with him from time to time, sometimes she had missed his company terribly.

She excitedly replied, "Sorry for some strange reason my phone was not working on roaming," and shared with him the story of what just happened at work.

Amir replied, "Yes I tried calling you today as I was expecting you back. I got worried about you. But don't worry. I will help you write a reply to your manager. We will sort it out."

Abeera's manager had committed promoting her to 'Floor manager'. But he said nothing and introduced the new 'floor manager' to her before the weekend. And now the manager didn't want to miss the opportunity of noting Abeera's irresponsible behavior.

And here it was, another issue to deal with. Abeera got disappointed again. *All I have is this job to support myself, and if I lose it, then what?* Even the thought scared Abeera.

Abeera reminds herself, *God is with me and God knows everything.*

So the next day, early in the morning, after discussing things with Amir.

Abeera wrote an explanation letter to the Human Resource manager.

Abeera's manager, in the meantime, sent an envelope to her, through his personal assistant.

Abeera opened the envelope, "Warning letter? Has he lost his mind?"

Angrily, she walked into his room, "You have no right to give me a warning letter!"

"I do," he replied, looking intensely at Abeera.

"No, you don't! The letter should come from Human Resources since the General Manager and Human Resource Manager are involved in the matter. Now I will not communicate to you on this matter. You highlighted it, and we will resolve it. It's no more between you and me."

The manager replied, "Well, I am your manager."

"I don't care. You could have waited for a day, but you didn't. I was not in Dubai and you knew it. It was my Saturday day off. I know why you created a scene out of this. Now, will you tear this letter, or do you want me to file a case against you in the Dubai Court with all the evidence of my day off? And then it will prove that you have unnecessarily created a scene. I am very courageous, and if it's a professional war you want, then come, let's fight and see who wins. Don't forget this is not Pakistan where you can do whatever you want to. This is Dubai, and if I complain, then the whole management will have to bear the mess because of this issue you have highlighted. So, don't hold me accountable, then!" Abeera was uncontrollably angry.

The manager became scared. He tore up the letter spontaneously. (Abeera laughed inside.) *What a coward he was! He was wrong, and I was ever ready to stand up for myself.*

In the afternoon Abeera went to the Human Resource office and handed over the letter of explanation in person. The Human Resource Manager smiled and said, "The manager is silly. It's such a petty issue. We will take care of this matter, don't worry."

The Human Resource Manager also responded to the manager's email by saying they would take care of the matter and there should be no further exchange of emails between Abeera and her manager.

Abeera's manager put her on the evening shifts to avoid interactions with her. He also deliberately did this so she could not achieve her targets as in the evenings very few customers visited the bank.

Chapter 5

The Abuse

Both personal and professional lives were now out of control of Abeera.

Abeera was efficient, committed, and hardworking at work. Many managers admired her. Some bosses would even say she didn't need a supervisor. But this manager was the strangest.

Abeera was falling below targets in the evening. Evening shifts brought their own challenges. Because there was less staff available she could not complete the work that needed support from other departments. She also had to call her manager several times when she needed his approval.

However, only a short while after the incident, the manager became depressed himself. He was due for a promotion, but he didn't get promoted. So, deep inside, Abeera should have been happy because of his frustration. He was not a supportive manager. He was unfair to her and now he felt his boss was unfair to him. God was granting justice. Abeera realized we often make commitments which we can't keep and then comes the cruel reality, which we fail to face. Instead of choosing to be honest about the situation at hand, we look for ways to avoid it.

But one-day Abeera spoke with the manager's wife when she came to the bank. There she explained to Abeera, "Actually my husband had to promote the other person because the management had hired him and now my husband was feeling bad about not promoting you. He is feeling embarrassed to speak about the situation with you."

Abeera smiled and thanked her for the explanation.

Abeera told herself, *sometimes you need compassion. If you can understand the other person's position, it becomes easy to let go.*

Abeera was no longer disappointed at what her manager had done to her.

For a few months,

Abeera would sit outside a nearby mall, listen to old music, and weep. Sometimes she would drink over the weekend. She understood how some women (especially mothers at least in the east), become so insecure after their son gets married. She felt deserted and lonely.

Interestingly, she became friends with her sister-in-law and took care of her as a sister. Even though it was because of her that she had so many issues at home. Saima and Abeera were meeting often. Saima argued with Abeera that her relationships had changed only because of her sister-in-law. All Abeera replied was, "If these relationships were strong, no force on Earth could have changed them. That poor girl had nothing to do with it. She made me see the reality of my relationships I was so proud of. I should rather be thankful to her."

June 2014

It was just a few months in their marriage. Moiz and his wife were arguing and fighting every day. Moiz would get drunk every night and often beat his wife. Their fights became so violent that Abeera's father and Sohail tactfully asked them to visit Lahore.

It terrified everybody because if the police caught Moiz drunk, they would put him behind bars and the family would have to pay a huge price to get him released. In Sharjah, there was no leniency for alcohol.

After Moiz reached Lahore, his wife went to her family's place and his family forced Moiz to divorce his wife. He was under so much pressure that he signed the papers of divorce.

After signing the divorce papers, Abeera's brother asked their mother to visit UAE soon.

One week after. Moiz changed his mind. His only concern was now his wife. He didn't care about anyone. He told everyone, "My wife is very important for me, the divorce is not valid, and I have patched up with my wife again. My wife was pregnant when I divorced her. As per Islamic laws, the divorce is not valid if the wife is pregnant."

The mother had now reached UAE, she spoke to Moiz. She suspected Moiz's wife was doing magic to get hold of their son completely. But Moiz completely rejected his mother's accusation and replied, "It is my life, I am not divorcing my wife, no matter what. If you want to stay with me. Please do. Otherwise, you can leave. I am sorry."

Eventually, Abeera's father and Sohail decided that Abeera and her mother should move out (This time they didn't ask Abeera to leave) and that nobody would contact Moiz.

Abeera moved out with her mother. The move became easy because of her mother's help. Abeera searched for the most convenient place possible and found a big room to rent where she could pay monthly and leave when things would resolve with Moiz.

Abeera's mother returned to Lahore after staying with Abeera for one month. She was very upset that Moiz's wife had done magic on him. Abeera didn't believe her mother either but she felt the weird energy when she was living with her brother. And because of that, she had now become fearful of living alone. But she ignored it. She thought it was because of all the emotional issues that had been going on in her life with her relationships.

Abeera was disappointed with these issues in the family. When her father had abandoned her she felt emotionally shattered. Now his own son, Moiz had done the same to him. Asking him to compromise with his son's decision or leave him. Abeera could witness that God was granting justice again. She believed God always grant justice. But no matter what, it was painful for her. She wanted no one to go through that pain she had faced. But inside she felt much more stable.

Abeera's father was now talking to her. He was very disappointed with Moiz's behavior with the family. Abeera still wanted to ease her father's pain, and she told him, "Don't worry, whatever you need, I am here, as always." Abeera got this immense power to have compassion and show kindness even to the people who had hurt her.

Abeera spent a few months living alone. Everyone in the family continued to be very upset because of Moiz.

Abeera too was in pain, and very fearful. But no one had an interest in knowing what had been going on with her? They all thought she had no worries because she lived in Dubai or just because she had a well-paid job, everything was perfect in her life. Again despite all the hurt caused by his brother to her, Abeera would still miss her brother a lot and cry but no one knew.

December 2014

Months passed.

Abeera's father visited Dubai and stayed with her for a month. They weren't on talking terms with Moiz.

Abeera feared her father as she didn't trust him anymore. The more he was with her, the more she became fearful. The last time he asked her to leave was still on her mind. She tried not to think more about that. *But how do you trust someone who can kick you out of their lives despite a 30-year bond?* She asked herself.

Yet Abeera took regular care of her father and took him to visit places. They spent New Year's Eve together enjoying the celebrations at the World's Tallest Tower, the Burj Khalifa. They went to Abu Dhabi with the help of a colleague who was also traveling to watch the cricket match with his family. Her father really enjoyed watching cricket in the stadium.

She took him to Fujairah too. Fujairah city is one of the seven states of UAE. It is a city full of mountains with amazing mosques and beautiful white sandy beaches. It took a few hours for them to reach by bus in the morning. They spent a day and came back to Dubai in the night.

In Dubai, Abeera took her father to the Global Village—claimed to be the world's largest leisure/shopping and entertainment project. And on every weekday she would take her father to Dubai Marina or JBR for dinner or they enjoyed Pakistani tea which her father loved.

She was taking care of him as before but the most cherished daughter/father bond was no more.

After a month, Abeera's father went back to Lahore.

The next day Abeera's eldest sister Nigar called Abeera and informed her, "Sohail and dad are planning to sell off the house which you have paid for and starting a business together. The market had been booming and the cost of the house had increased tremendously.

"And our father had changed his mind. He is now talking to Moiz, again. If they leave him, all his money will be for his wife.

"Only you are a loser, living on our own without the family. Everyone is friends with Moiz now. And dad doesn't need you now. You have paid for the house and they will never transfer the papers in your name and if you insist they will break ties with you. It's all about money. I am glad I am married and settled with my husband.

"It is unfortunate to live with a father like him, we were much better off without him. I feel sorry for you."

Abeera did not believe Nigar and replied, "Let me come to Lahore and deal with the matter."

Abeera was wondering, *dad has savings, the support of Sohail and also herself. Then why would he want to sell the house and start a business?*

Since Abeera's father didn't tell her anything about his planning to sell the house, she got worried. She decided she would go to Lahore and get the papers transferred in her name, as per her father's commitment so that this chapter would be closed for good.

If Abeera lost her job in Dubai, she could go back to Pakistan and have a place to stay.

Abeera went to Saima's mother. She shared with her the story of what was happening now with the house. She was in the kitchen. While pouring food into the dish she replied to Abeera, "By now you should have gotten married. Then this nasty never-ending drama in your family would not have bothered you as rightly your sister mentioned."

Abeera replied to her aunt, "I wonder how people get into relationships and don't lose themselves, unlike me. I keep clinging to the one I get close to, and then, one day, out of the blue, I feel suffocated and want my freedom back. I don't understand. Relationships are not meant for me. I am fed up with trying my luck again and again. I give up. Is there a way of success in relationships? I always thought somebody would come and understand the real 'me' with my pure loving heart and we would get married. Isn't that how it should be? That happens in movies and romance novels. But here it seems every man wants to take advantage of me. How do I get married to a man who only wants a physical thing? I mean, I don't understand. They can find many women in bars and clubs who they can sleep with. Why me?"

The aunt while serving Abeera food replied, "Do not dwell too much into that. Life is full of challenges for everyone. Focus on the good things in your life and be grateful to God. God is with you. Do not worry. But your father had committed to transfer the papers in your name than what happened. Did you speak to him again?"

"I have paid for it. But I have no right over it. And look at my parents, who can live in my house but never accept it. They lie and tell everyone that Moiz has paid for the house even though he had only contributed 10 percent. I wonder what is so wrong in a daughter paying for the house. I had never recognized that their insecurities could become so unbearable."

The aunt nodded in agreement, "I can understand it. Logically speaking people are insecure in the East. We don't have old-age benefits. And besides a daughter paying for the parent's house is a shame for them."

"I never asked them to vacate the house. Why are they worried about old age? They can live as long as they want to. And that is what my father had agreed to when I paid for it. I wonder why they have become so insecure. My parents were always fair in their dealings as much as I remember. I had always admired them. What is the difference between a son paying and the daughter paying? I don't get it. It is ridiculous; I live in a mess, a complete mess. A family full of double standards and inequalities. It's sheer madness." Abeera answered while taking the first bite of the food.

"I don't think your mother has anything to do with it. Of what you have told me, it's your father who takes decisions." The aunt replied.

"Yes, but my mother can still speak up for what is fair and just," Abeera answered taking a sip from her glass.

"Anyway, don't worry about how you can make more money. God is the biggest compensator. You can make more money. Enjoy your freedom in Dubai."

"Yes, I have freedom here that is true. Back home they focus so much on what I wear. Where is your scarf? They always ask. And if I am not covered properly, it means I am characterless. I don't get it. I mean, if by wearing a scarf I can prove I am a woman of high character, then I pity their thinking. Going out with my friends have always been another issue. If hanging out with boys makes me a characterless woman, I pity their mind-sets. All they want is that I get married.

For them, a girl should get married the moment she reaches puberty. I can have no life on my own." Abeera said in her frustrated tone.

"Well! You are right but few girls think like this in Pakistan. Though some girls have raised these questions. I must say you are very different and very courageous." The aunt replied.

"Being different is so challenging. Are there any different people like me on this earth? I don't understand why God made me this way. Here I am, almost 31, and I still have no control over my life. My sisters got married when they were 22, why didn't I?"

"You had other goals. You wanted to study. You wanted to become independent. No?" The aunt replied.

"That is true but we women in the East are never independent. Just by making money and getting a job one doesn't get independence. In fact, it troubles us more. My friends back home think I have a long list of boyfriends. The impression in a Pakistani society of a single lady, living alone is the same. They think I have nothing else to do than change boyfriends like clothes, party, drink, throw up, and that's all my life is about." Abeera replied.

"I understand your frustration. But you don't have to let these things trouble you. Live your life the way you want to. It is your life. Nobody has the right to dictate your life other than yourself." The aunt replied.

"I have a well-paid job, but I had realized earlier that money can't buy you peace, love, and happiness. If happiness comes from money, I would have been happy today."

"You are right. When you have money, you get to know the realities of many people and their relationships. Money is a 'means' like all other things in life."

"But I am a failure; I have failed repeatedly in my life. My life is nothing but a failure. Where am I headed to? Here I am still trying to sort out my life." Abeera said shrugging her shoulders.

"Where am I headed to? That is a great question, to begin with. Now you have asked the right questions, God will answer you. The first step is to accept your mistakes and learn from them. Mistakes are an opportunity to learn," The aunt explained to her.

"I don't deny that I made many mistakes in life. But I had always taken ownership of my life, even when I felt lost. I had control over myself. I realized that the only person you have control over is yourself. And whenever I can sort my inner contradictions, gradually the peace arises, and I become peaceful." Abeera replied.

"But that is a constant work. Never stop revisiting your inner self. Always spend time with yourself and know your inner state." The aunt argued.

"I learned this earlier. After my breakup. But it is such hard work all the time." Abeera replied in a low voice burdened by the remembrance of all the hardship.

"That is life. Life is not a straight road. Life is full of bumpy roads. And because of these phases, you can learn and grow. Otherwise, life would be displeasing and meaningless." The aunt explained.

"I know but I wonder when my life will change? I am a failure at everything: a failure in the eyes of myself, a failure in the eyes of my family, a failure in my friends' opinion and maybe a failure in God's opinion. I would rather go see a psychologist. I beat the drum of being happily single, but I am not happy with life. All I do is go to work then come home and sleep. Is this life? I have no savings. In fact, I have to pay off my loan and I am still looking for what is the purpose of my life." Abeera replied.

"There is nothing wrong with being a failure if that is what you think. But let me tell you. You are never a failure in God's opinion, as long as you keep turning to God, God helps you. You only fail God when you fail yourself." The aunt replied while she walks into the kitchen.

"Are you saying I didn't fail myself?" Abeera asked in a state of confusion while she was following the aunt.

"No, you fail yourself only when you give up on yourself. You are still seeking answers to your questions when many people at this stage might become frustrated and give up." The aunt clarified.

"Thank you, aunty, for clarifying. The more I question the more I have learned about myself. It is difficult as sometimes it takes tremendous courage." She replied.

The aunt was very pleased with Abeera and replied, "Be courageous. Having courage is a very important aspect of life."

"Ok, aunty." Abeera thanked the aunt and left.

The next day,

Things in Abeera's professional life got better. The Human Resource Manager called Abeera and suggested transferring her to the Barsha branch as per banks job rotation policy.

The Barsha branch was at a superb location and its customers were affluent. Abeera was certain she would love it, but she refused as it was too far from her residence.

She asked the Human Resource Manager if they could transfer her to another branch that was closer to where she has recently shifted. The Human Resource Manager agreed.

God is so kind. In some parts of Abeera's life, she could witness that.

Abeera was now working with one of her favorite managers. He was the first manager she had worked with. He was appreciative and supportive of her and she was very comfortable with him. She could now foresee that the next couple of years would be easy, career-wise.

That night Abeera thanked God. Abeera made it a practice to thank God for the smallest of things God had given her. She wrote:

Oh! God,
Thank you very much, God
For being with me in all this time.

Thank you very much, God
For taking care of me.

Thank you very much, God
For all the blessings.

Thank you very much, God
For helping me

Thank you very much, God
For providing me

Thank you very much, God
For protecting me

Thank you very much, God
For everything, you have given me.

And no matter how much I thank you God, it will still not be enough.

March 2015

Abeera went to Pakistan. Sadness remained deeply rooted inside her. She had to call the lawyer herself and get the papers ready in her name. All her life, she had hidden nothing from her father. He always knew her salary, her friends, her routines, her customers, her experiences, and everything. She never took the credit for who she had become. She believed all that she had gained in life was because of her parents. Abeera again asked her father to get the papers signed in her name. Her father said, "Let the papers in your mother's name come from the lawyer and then we will sign the papers for you. Don't worry."

"But I have the papers ready with me." Abeera replied.

"You can leave them with me for your next visit." He replied.

Abeera said, "Ok."

Abeera's father was singing an old song and laughing with a sarcastic look on his face, "When my own loved ones ditched me, a stranger helped me."

This time again he was behaving strangely. Abeera noticed it but could not understand what was going on.

Abeera prayed day in and day out, "God, why is my father acting so distant? All my life he had supported me. But what happened to him today?"

While Abeera was sitting in the living room and could not help her tears flow. Her sister saw her crying and asked her why she was crying and if she was missing Dubai?

Abeera remained silent and told herself, *Home is a place where people who connect from the heart live. In my room in Dubai, I only see walls around me, and even with my family, it seems a place full of strangers. It seems as if I am at someone else's home. I feel like a stranger with my own loved ones.*

These few days were very difficult. At every second, it felt as if the family was plotting something against Abeera. They all had an eye on her. Wherever she would go, her sister would accompany her. She would even listen to her calls when Abeera was on the phone. It was suffocating. Abeera could see how everyone in the family had changed.

Ameen told Abeera, "You are stupid and what Nigar had told you is right. Remember when you broke up with Daniyal, what Savera told you. She said you should not worry about the breakup as Daniyal had spent alot of money on you. You should have known these people by now. All they want is money and all that matters to them is money. They have no humanity. They didn't care about you crying in pain after your breakup. You still expect these people to be sincere with you?"

Abeera in her helpless voice replied to Ameen, "It can be true. But what happened to my father?"

Ameen replied, "He is under their influence. Savera and Sohail."

Abeera acknowledged, "Maybe, but I am only concerned about my father. He is not a baby boy who can come under anyone's influence."

The Abuse

Ameen told her with confidence, "One day you will trust me on this. And I know that day is not very far. You will know the truth of these relationships soon."

Soon it was time for Abeera to go back to Dubai. On the last day, Abeera's father mentioned to her, "The eldest son had already cut off ties with us. Now I can't afford to cut off ties with Moiz. We have rights over him and the money he makes. I will call him now. Please talk to him."

Abeera shockingly asked, "But you cut off ties with Moiz because of religious matters. He patched up with his wife even after divorcing her. Wasn't this the reason? How can you change your mind today?"

Her father denied, "I have consulted many Muslim Scholars, and some of them have advised me I should not leave my son as I have the right over his money."

Abeera was again upset with her father. He was using religion for the money he wanted from his son.

Nonetheless, Abeera spoke to her brother.

The next day Abeera travelled back to Dubai. It seemed as if her father had really wanted her to leave. Abeera could open a locker for herself in the bank and put her jewellery in the locker. She took many years to save money and buy jewellery for herself, and here she doesn't seem to trust anybody. Tomorrow these people might sell her gold and there she would think again, *Am I careless, irresponsible, or a failure?*

Although her trip helped her organize her jewellery, Abeera realized that this money and these material things would be of no good if you are not happy inside. Her father had already kicked her out once and anything could happen again. And now she trusted no one.

Abeera told herself, *my friends are enjoying their lives in Pakistan and I am here struggling between relationships, trying to protect myself, as if they are my biggest enemies.*

After a week.

Moiz called Abeera. It was still March 2015. He had a baby girl. Abeera was happy for him. Abeera booked the flight over the weekend again and visited them.

Abeera had planned a few hours visit to Lahore to avoid unnecessary confrontations. Besides, the home was not a peaceful place anymore.

Abeera landed in Lahore in the early morning and told no one about her trip. She asked a friend to pick her up from the airport. He then dropped her at her place. Everyone was sleeping. They woke up with the doorbell when she rang the bell.

They shared the same stories of how disappointed they were with Moiz's wife. Nobody was talking to his wife.

Yet Abeera went to her sister-in-law's house even when nobody wanted to go. She enjoyed with the little angel, took pictures and posted them on social media.

This was the shortest visit of Abeera to her family. She was flying back to Dubai the same night. She only wanted to share the moments of happiness with her family.

Abeera returned to Dubai. It was early morning on Saturday. The war in Yemen had only added fuel to the fire. Abeera heard the UAE rulers saying that if Pakistan didn't support them, they would pay a huge price. There was panic in the Pakistani community in UAE.

Abeera's fears were coming to the surface with each passing day. Abeera told herself, "God is with me. I should not worry about the future and trust God."

Abeera became worried about her brother who might divorce his wife again anytime. He was struggling to make the two families happy. His wife was beautiful, and she was now a successful model. Savera didn't like her and not only Savera but nobody in the family liked her. She was outspoken as Abeera, and men in Abeera's family wanted to control the women whether it was a wife, a daughter, or a daughter-in-law. Last time the family had pressurized Moiz to divorce his wife and they might want to do that again.

April 2015

It was EID in two months' time. Abeera excitedly planned her visit to Lahore for EID. She bought expensive gifts for everyone as usual: lovely outfits for the kids, shirts for all the men, and perfume for all the women.

But, her plans didn't work. Her father called. He asked for money to pay taxes due on the house. Abeera replied, "I am coming in a few days and we will pay for it together. I also need to get the papers signed in my name, remember?"

Before Abeera even finished her sentence, her father in his loud voice replied, "Who the hell do you think you are? Just because you are wealthy, you think so highly of yourself. I am not dependent on you. You should depend on me!"

Abeera barely understood what he said, "What do you mean?" Abeera responded, hesitatingly.

"I meant you think you are smart. Do whatever you can and bring whoever you want but we won't transfer the papers in your name!"

Abeera shockingly replied, "Dad, you are being unfair. We mutually agreed last time when I came to Lahore. And even before I paid for the house, you agreed to transfer the papers in my name."

Her father was extremely angry. He didn't care. He continued, "I am your father and I can do anything. You don't have to remind me of what I am supposed to do. Last time when you came, I didn't know what to answer." Then he was abusive, "Fuck off and go to hell. You and your money!" he yelled.

That was the last thing Abeera expected. But after all that had happened last time, it did not surprise Abeera. However, her father was being abusive that she couldn't tolerate.

Abeera replied boldly, "Ok, dad, so what's the point of this so-called relationship, if that's the case? I sort of knew whenever I would stand up for my rights, I will have to face your insecurities. You got what you wanted and you don't need me anymore. It's clear now. You have already disrespected and insulted me many times before and this time you have crossed the line. I won't accept your abuse no matter what, learn to respect your daughter first."

To which he responded, "Who are you to decide that? I will decide. You are from me. I am not from you."

Trying to control anger, Abeera replied, "I am not deciding. I am just stating the truth. You keep disrespecting me again, and again. This time I will not tolerate your abuse. No one has the right to abuse me. Even if it's you."

"Get lost! We don't want to have any relationship with you, neither me nor anyone else!" Her father yelled.

Abeera replied, "Fine. I expected that from you."

The call ended on a terrible note. Abeera wished there were laws to protect children from the abuse and injustices of their parents in the East.

Abeera went to the balcony, looked at the sky, *we muslims place parents on a very high pedestal and as they say, parents are God-like. Parents can do anything with total impunity. Is this what God would do to His people, people who love Him?*

Abeera came back into the room after 20 minutes wiping her tears. She picked up a paper and wrote a letter to God:

Oh! God, lord of the worlds!
I know ——that you know everything. You even know the state of the hearts. You know the pain and agony I am going through. Not only tears are flowing from my eyes but my heart is also crying.
I had never complained. Never complained about anything to You.

THE GIRL WHO LOVED HERSELF

In childhood when we had nothing to eat I would sleep empty stomach.

When all my school friends would enjoy the snacks in the break time and I had no money I patiently looked at them.

And when I grew old, men harassed me at work.

At home my life was miserable.

And my love life, so many men I fell in love but my love life remained a failure.

Life was never easy. But I didn't complain.

I asked for Your help and kept fighting with all the difficulties, failures and thorns of my life.

I am still not complaining; You are the Lord of the world, who am I to complain. But I am here, helpless, restless and hopeless.

All the past wounds seem smaller to what had happened today.

Do parents hurt children? And I am here specifically talking about my father. My own father. Who I loved and adored. He also claimed to love me.

The man who betrayed me, fooled me, abused me, and abandoned me, is no one else other than my father?

God, no man in this world has ever spoken to me like this.

But, I don't have the courage to take revenge from my father.

God, what difficulty have You put me in? I can never be happy if I hurt my father.

God, You know I have spent 30 years in the love of my father.

And what have I not done for him?

God, You know everything.

Since when was he fooling me I don't know?

Reality is cruel. Who should I blame: myself, my father or money? For the first time in my life, I have accepted that my father is a liar, a hypocrite who only uses his children for his own needs.

But when anyone insults me and abuses me. I can't tolerate. I learned all my life to respect myself, to love myself. And today on one side is a valley and on the other side is a river and whichever path I choose it is only me who is at a loss. Loss of a self or loss of a father.

God, what shall I do that everything would go back to normal?

You are the God, God who does wonders, who does miracles.

You never leave anyone empty-handed, who turns to you. You listen to everyone. I plead. I plead and I am here to appeal, for Your mercy.

God, I know, I have done nothing for You. Neither have I prayed 5 times nor have I fasted in the month of Ramadan nor have I done anything for you. But I have loved myself very much. I kept my heart away from all the malice.

The Abuse

    The honesty and the sincerity in my heart had never allowed me to lie, cheat, betray or hurt anyone.
    God, please, don't leave me alone. Please don't leave me ever alone. If You also leave me, who will I go to?
    Oh God! please give peace to my heart and my soul.
    Your faithful,
    Abeera

Abeera wrote a poem:

I am the light; I am the darkness,
I create my world where ever I go;
I am a whole where ever I am,
O my lover, O my lover
When you dump your trash on me
I experience nothing but who I am,
And who I am is much stronger than I can ever know

I am not scared of the darkness
I fear the light that shines through me
when you abandon me; I am left with a broken me
Yet I promise you, I will join all the torn parts again
Transcend and rebuild who I am
Oh, lover, I promise you, I will never give up.

Lessons we can learn from Abeera:

There is nothing more beautiful than living with integrity. She learned to have courage, the courage to stand up for herself. The courage to decide for herself. The courage to live life with integrity.

Doing things for others is wonderful but you must not neglect yourself.

Abeera learned that having standards for herself is very important.

There are several boundaries one must draw. Boundaries about physical, emotional, domestic and psychological violations. And no one should be allowed to cross those boundaries. Not even your parents.

Chapter 6

God And The Angels

Abeera went to her aunt, hugged her and shared the abuse of her father. With tears rolling down her cheeks, " Abeera said, "Aunty, I lived a life full of hatred, full of anger and frustration when I was young. But I have always been very honest. I have never lied to anyone. I have never cheated anyone, nor have I ever betrayed anyone. I wonder why all this is happening in my life. I was strong then and now I feel very weak and powerless. I don't know how to handle this. Before I used to think as you grow you become mature enough to handle everything life brings you. And here I am, incapable of handling all this."

The aunt replied while she started recitation using the beads in her hand, "Sometimes relationships fail when you get closer to God."

"And it seems everything is failing in my life." Abeera replied immediately and continued, "My respect comes first. I do not allow anyone to disrespect me. And today, I wish I can tell you my anguish."

"Oh, darling, this is only a 'means' and you don't complain with 'means'?" The aunt replied while she continued her recitation.

"'Means', what is 'means'? And my respect? They insulted me. I will not allow them to insult me."

"I told you. This is only a 'means'. And you don't complain with 'means'. They only made it easier for you to understand what God had decided for you. The matter of hearts is only with God." The aunt replied.

"I don't understand aunty but I will not allow any insult or abuse in my life."

Abeera went into the other room to sleep and said goodbye to the aunt.

Abeera stayed that night with her aunt. That night was again a night full of questions and Abeera had no answers to, *what was happening in her life? Would everything go back to where it was before? Would I be able to love my father as before?*

Abeera left in the morning.

After Moiz returned to Dubai, Abeera shared the story of what had happened the previous night on the phone with her father. To which he replied, "What can I do?"

Abeera hung up and told herself, *I still expect help from this family, it is stupid of me.*

May 2015

Every day was painful and full of challenges.

It was Shab E Barat (a big Islamic night).

Abeera stayed at her aunt's place again that night. They went out for dinner and to a beautiful mosque for night prayers.

That night was overwhelming, she couldn't help but cry. Abeera had spent so many days and nights crying she was wondering how she could still be alive. Abeera told her aunt, "What more can I face? God has given me too much to handle."

The aunt explained to Abeera, "God writes destinies tonight. You should ask for forgiveness."

Abeera said angrily, "We are puppets, our string is in God's hand."

The aunt became very annoyed, "If you want to have peace, surrender to the will of God. This is the will of God for you. The sooner you accept it, the sooner you will get your own peace."

"That is what I mean this is the will of God. To hurt me. To take away my relationships from me. The relationships I loved the most in my life. God is very unfair to me." Abeera replied.

"No, darling. We are sinners. We, humans, are very small. Who are we to question God? Don't rebel like the devil (Shaitaan)? God doesn't like people who rebel. Make His will your will. Everything will then be fine. This is the will of God for you. It is only God who can take away everything. God tests us through our loved ones. You should free yourself from yourself (NAFS-EGO)."

"Free myself from myself, how? Why would God do this to me? What wrong did I do?" Abeera asked.

"Your salvation will only be found after you accept the will of God. When you argue with the reality of your life you argue with God. Learn to accept God's will for you. God likes those who surrender and submit themselves to Him. Darling, let go, let go of what God has taken away from you. Do not resist."

That night Abeera prayed and cried, *"Please God have mercy on me, please, please. I plead I ask for mercy, I ask for peace. I ask for forgiveness. I am sorry. I know nothing. Only You know what is good for me."*

After a few days.

Moiz called Abeera and requested her, "Now I have a daughter and Dubai is very expensive. Can we live together again so we can share the rent?"

Abeera became angry. *Is he insane? He is so selfish and inconsiderate.* But she didn't let her anger take over her and calmly replied, "Let your wife come to Dubai. Then we will see."

Dubai was getting hotter day by day, and Abeera badly needed a car. It was the first day of Ramadan. She walked home from the metro. It was a ten minutes' walk but in the summers Dubai weather is terrible. The air conditioner in her room hadn't worked last night.

Abeera did not feel well. She had a severe cough. Often, she would wake up in the middle of the night and cough. Even her neighbors could hear her cough. But now she was sure that the Human Resource department had her number. If she died, UAE Government would send her dead body back to Pakistan then her family would bury her and they may forgive her.

All these nights in pain again reminded her that sometimes you have a family, yet you are all alone.

Many nights passed, crying. It was very difficult for Abeera to close her eyes and sleep, she would often see nightmares and a witch in her dreams. And when she closed her eyes to meditate, she felt the witch in the dreams was in her room and wanted to kill her. She could not meditate. Only God knew how she slept.

Some nights she would wake up from her dream of the witch. She was convinced that the witch will one day kill her and who knew if she would die and might not be alive tomorrow.

On the weekends she would visit her aunt's place and there she could relax. The witch was not appearing, and she could have a proper sleep.

June 2015

Abeera financed a car. Her brother was so busy with his life he could only give her two hours the previous weekend to visit a showroom.

It was her friend Amir who helped her to select a car and visit different showrooms with her.

Abeera's mother called her and asked her to visit them in Lahore. Abeera replied, "No, Mom. Dad will kill me. He is very annoyed. I don't understand why he got so upset with me. He himself agreed on the papers. I trusted him. He was the one who asked me to borrow a loan and pay for the house. Mom, I don't know why he is acting so strange now. What did I wrong? Please explain. I beg you."

Abeera's mother replied, "Your father is greedy. You should have not trusted him. You should have asked me. Why did you get the property transferred in my name? You should have gotten them transferred in your name the moment you sent the money. You were blinded with his love and that is why I never told you anything. Now keep this to yourself and come to Lahore. I will try to speak to your father."

It stunned Abeera, "Mom, how can you spend a life with such a man?"

"Abeera can you stop asking the same question again. I had told you before, we, Eastern women had no choice a few decades ago. However, you are independent. You can make your own choices. Do what you want to do with your life. But, me, I had nowhere else to go. After marriage, my parents' house was closed for me. I could only visit them as a guest. Divorce was a terrible affair, the society used to blame and curse the woman not the man." Abeera's mother replied.

"Ok, fine mom. But I am not coming to Lahore." Abeera replied.

It was the first week of Ramadan (Ramadan is the most blessed month for Muslims). Abeera came home with her new car. Abeera always loved her freedom and independence but the price she had to pay this time was the immense hurt and pain buried deep inside her soul.

Children were playing outside her apartment. They liked her car. Abeera thanked them, and came inside her room, looked in the mirror, kissed and told herself, "Congratulations on your brand-new car." This was the first celebration of her life where she didn't have her family to share her happiness with.

Abeera asked herself, if I pick up a paper again will God speak to me.

It was the first Ramadan of her life when she had Sehri (a pre-dawn meal for fasting) alone.

After having Sehri, she sat at the table in the balcony outside her room and looked at the sky, having her tea and told herself, *who knows the cost of this life? No one knows the real life. And what is real? What is an ideal life? Life is never perfect. God gives you one thing and then takes away something else.*

In the morning, Abeera drove to work. Everyone liked her car. This was the second brand-new car of her life. The first one she had bought was for her family. She never got an appreciation for that. Abeera came home in the afternoon from work. She parked her car and went to her room, took a shower and freshened up.

In the evening, she broke her fast and had dinner. Then she wore her big prayer gown and walked to the nearby mosque. It was a grand mosque, just five minutes' walk from the place where she lived. They had special arrangements for Ramadan's late night prayers.

The moment Abeera entered the mosque, she couldn't hold back her tears. There were immense blessings. Abeera felt at home. It seemed she had stepped right into God's house where she went for pilgrimage. During the whole prayer, she wept and prayed, *I only want you God, I only want You, God. I only need You, God. I ask for help. I ask for mercy. I ask for your support. Please save me. I submit myself to You, God. I have nobody except You, God and You have the power to protect me and save my life. God, Please. Please. Please.*

Every night Abeera would go to pray at the mosque. She felt peace in her heart through prayer. Through submission. Through acceptance. She wrote true

THE GIRL WHO LOVED HERSELF

love is:

The surrender to the will of God.
The acceptance of what God has given you.
The faith in God when things are falling apart.
The trust that God will save you no matter what.

At the mosque, Abeera made a new friend. She was married and often came to the mosque with her husband. The love of this couple was amazing. Abeera was really pleased. They both would take care of each other. Abeera smiled and thought, *for so long I had desired a loving relationship, but now I have no desires left.*

After a few nights, when Abeera headed to the mosque for prayers, she looked at the sky. The night had brought peace of mind and tranquillity of soul. She felt peaceful inside and outside her heart. She went inside the mosque, and during the whole prayer, she cried, again.

She made many supplications for several people, for her childhood friends, her school friends, her neighbours, past neighbours, colleagues, her grandparents, her relatives, people who she knew had died, for her parents and for herself.

It was surprising for her. Abeera never had a big list of supplications. She trusted that God would do the best for her as He had already given her so much. She thanked God more rather than asking for a list of desires.

Over the past few years since her breakup with Daniyal, Abeera had acknowledged how merciful God had been to her.

The night passed praying and crying. Finally, she could breathe in peace completely.

She shared her experience with her aunt who replied that in one night of Ramadan, "God sends angels and that is why she might have felt it so different and so peaceful."

It surprised Abeera, and she replied to her, "What? Me and angels? No, no, that's not possible. I am a bad girl; I fought with my father. My father does not like me anymore. I had illicit sexual encounters. I didn't respect my body. I have been drinking alcohol. There must be the pious people for whom God sends angels. My name wouldn't be anywhere close to theirs."

The aunt explained, "God speaks to people who have a pure heart. If the heart is clean and pure and filled with good deeds, anyone can experience God within themselves."

Abeera's family had never told her this, "What did you say, aunt?" It confused her.

The aunt explained, "God is for everyone and God is everywhere. He is talking to everyone all the time. The question is, who remembers Him?"

Abeera asked, "If God is everywhere, why people go to holy places?"

"To know God, to feel God, to be intimate with God, one does not have to go to the mountains, or to holy places, though these places can boost your inner state. But God is here, right here with you. The question is: 'Have you built your relationship with God? Can you feel Him? Can you talk to Him?'" The aunt replied.

"Can humans talk to God?" Abeera asked in surprise.

"God speaks to his people through their hearts." The aunt replied.

"Are you saying God is within us? Not separate from us, very near to us?" Abeera asked.

"Yes. God is not separate from us. The essence of God is in our hearts. Though we have veils between God and us on the physical level; on the level of the human body that does not mean God is separate from us. A heart awakened in the love of God is the richest heart in the world!" The aunt explained.

All her life Abeera had many misconceptions about God. Abeera believed God was only for the pious or God-fearing people. Beliefs like God likes a certain people and He will throw the rest in hell fire. Abeera was informed that there is a list of do's and don'ts that God wanted humans to follow.
The aunt also told Abeera, "There is no grander worldly experience than to experience God."

Ramadan passed quickly. This was her first Ramadan in Dubai that she made the most of it: she was going to many places to break her fast, enjoy pre-dawn meals and she performed her prayers regularly throughout the entire month of Ramadan.

But what really stood out was the uniqueness of that one special night. It was still unbelievable. *Is God for everyone? Even for me? Am I worthy? Has God given me attention?* Abeera couldn't believe that.

On the last night of Ramadan, Abeera did shopping for EID. It had been a few years Abeera had not celebrated. After shopping, Abeera received a call at midnight from her brother. And then, to her surprise, her elder sister Savera called as well. But all Abeera said was, "Thank you for calling and remembering my birthday."

July 2015
Abeera's birthday, the day of EID and Friday. Three occasions together. (Friday is the most blessed day of the week for Muslims).

Amir wanted to surprise Abeera. He went to Abeera and presented her a birthday gift and brought a cake with him. They cut the cake together and then went to a mall nearby, took photos, and had dinner. All her friends wished her happy birthday on social media. The day was beautiful both inside her heart and on the outside.

After Amir left, Abeera went to Saima's place to give her birthday cake.

The next few days were the best days of her life. Abeera connected with some old and some new friends. She would hang out regularly and write several notes.

Then so many things happened, more than she could have imagined. One surprise and then another. A friend proposed Abeera to marry him, which she didn't expect. All her new friends were nice and caring. This was a genuine form of friendship with men that Abeera had wished for all her life. None of them was 'friends with benefits.'

Gradually, she gained confidence again. Though, everything had changed in her life, her expectations and her perceptions.

At work, her bosses constantly praised her. Her name appeared on the list of top performers a few times. Her ex-manager was now praising Abeera in the meetings.

Her friends would ask her: "Are you lucky, or you are doing something special?"

All she would say is, "I meditate," and then burst into laughter.

Before she could understand it, even more, good appeared in her life. She labelled her friends, *He is my mentally connected friend, he is my spiritually connected friend, he is my lovely companion, and he is my Skype friend.* She connected with all of them so beautifully.

Abeera went to miracle garden one evening with an old university friend. She looked gorgeous wearing a beautiful pair of jeans with a blue T-shirt.

Abeera meditated regularly now. The peace that she got from silence was more important to her than the reasoning of her mind. Meditation had this immense power which logic can't have. Meditation helped her in self-acceptance and bringing awareness.

After doing regular meditation, Abeera felt activity in her heart like light, expansion, sensations or other manifestations in her life. It was a unique experience, hard to describe with words. Her thinking pattern and her attitude towards life, God and relationships changed.

She observed that meditation had the following benefits:

She became aware – aware of her thoughts and feelings.

She experienced closeness to the Divine, the Creator.
She felt a sense of peace arising within her.
She experienced subtle changes in her physical body.
Her attachment to materialist things and worldly matters reduced.

Lessons we can learn from Abeera:

There will be moments in your life when everything can change in just a matter of a few days, a few words or a few minutes. But never let any of those forget 'who you are'. Be yourself even in those moments.

Abeera realized: When you go against yourself you lose the relationship with yourself. When you love yourself you build on your relationship with yourself.

Don't worry about the medium you use to connect to God. Talk to God through letters or talk to God in prayers. God will know the purity of your heart.

Time never remains the same nor do people nor relationships. But God's love for you never changes.

Life is a process of both the highs and the lows, do not resist the process. Let the time of discomfort pass.

No matter how terrible the events of your life make you feel in reality they are only an opportunity for your own grander understanding.

Don't indulge in thoughts like you cannot be close to God or God is for some people or God requires a list of things from you. Rather involve God in everything like you involve your best friend. In the matters of happiness, In the matters of sorrows, in the matters of uncertainty, and in all the matters of your life.

Search for the greater meaning in life and the meaning will appear.

In life, everything is connected. Bless every moment and bless every relation.

Resistance to life at any given moment is resistance to God's will for you.

Abeera realized: Turn to God and see wonders happen in your life.

Chapter 7

The Healing

Abeera received a call from Farhan, who she had met in Singapore. Farhan was moving to Australia and was planning to come to Dubai to visit his sister and relatives.

Farhan offered dinner to Abeera at one of her favorite Chinese cuisine "P F Chang's".

Farhan reached Dubai and soon they met at the restaurant. After the restaurant, they spent the night together watching movies and discussing. Abeera shared her self-discoveries with Farhan. He knew that Abeera was still holding onto a lot of baggage.

In the morning, Farhan said he had to tell her something but he would write it in an email and send it to her later that week.

After a few days, Abeera received the following email:

From: Farhan Ahmed
Date: Aug 22, 2015 6:13
Subject: Exploring Abeera
To: Abeera Shaikh

Hello Abeera,

Hope you are doing well and enjoying the journey to self-discovery. I was very pleased to see you moving forward in the right direction. I am glad you shared quite a lot with me, but what you didn't, I have addressed it in this email, after much deliberation. I have written the truth in its complete entirety to shed light on your multiple complex issues. I hope you will take them positively and be a master of yourself rather than feeling pity. I also hope this email will help you further on your journey to self-mastery.

Are you ready for it?

A long time ago there was a girl. She was brought up in a backward area of a country in the early 1980's. It was a conservative country, and she didn't want much: some simple things in life and to settle one day with a family of her own. She couldn't wait to grow up and live her dream life. Then, some unsavoury things happened, like sexual abuse. A trusted person took advantage of the girl and scared her. The girl, in the beginning, got scared of the whole sex thing and went off in that direction. She didn't know how to counter the feelings of anxiety, horror, and shame.

Her clueless family couldn't understand her reaction and her behavior. They were puzzled. Instead of giving her the care and concern she always needed, they made her life miserable.

The Healing

She was always looking for an escape – somehow, somewhere it would work.

Then came the real tragedy.

The loving, caring people who wanted to be with her she considered them fools and boring and pushed them away. The problem worsened when certain men who had no shame or maturity took it as a challenge. They persisted and she allowed these men to enter her life.

These people only looked for a good time. The result was a disaster, a complete shock. They consumed her and left her. To survive, she adopted the values and rules which these people lived by. She indulged in things like smoking, drinking, clubbing, and physical relationships. She always hoped it would fill that hole unknowingly that gap inside herself.

Some years passed.

The problem had become worse. Now she was financially and physically well, but inside she was still alone and couldn't understand why she kept meeting immature assholes. Her family still didn't understand her.

She never even for a second realized that her own perceptions were distorted. She had adopted the values according to what she had sensed in her family, "To let yourself be used, dominated and insulted."

In principle, these values are the opposite of how it should be. Unknowingly she was trying to convince herself that she was strong, a feminist, independent, and free-spirited.

Her behaviors were uncertain and confusing, even to herself. But she never revisited her perceptions.

She had convinced herself that on the surface she is tough and strong and that she is fine. That's why she continued with her bad addictions.

The biggest proof of this is: she cried, she wept. She cried all the tears she had hidden inside, for NOT being used, dominated or insulted, when for the first time in 15 years she got treated as an equal, as an adult, as someone worthy of respect by a 24-year-old friend (Me).

The proof continues: The next morning, she tried to dismiss the experience as something odd. She tried to forget it, but just couldn't stop wondering. What the hell had she experienced? Is it true? Is she worth it? Did she deserve it? How should she deal with it?

Perhaps the biggest proof is that if she was all hard, tough, and free-spirited, she wouldn't have cried. That experience with me would not have bothered her.

THE GIRL WHO LOVED HERSELF

She would not have come to the airport in the evening to see off this guy who touched her soul.

BUT SHE DID... This means she is not how she portrays herself.

So what are you waiting for?

THE MOST IMPORTANT THING YOU HAVE BEEN WAITING TO HEAR:

You are courageous; you are very strong. You have suffered a lot. Your entire life almost got spoilt. But enough, no more. Your suffering ends now. It's over. Here is the acknowledgement you always wanted. Here are the words you always wanted to hear. It's time for you to be at rest and at peace with yourself. You are beautiful. Please don't torture yourself and give in to your dirty habits. Please, stop punishing yourself. You deserve love, respect and care. Don't give up. Don't resign yourself to your fate.

We request and beg for your apology. Please, don't torture yourself like a fat man does by eating more, like a drug addict does by doing more drugs. Stop feeding your bad and dirty habits. We want you. Please, be the real you. You will get the family, life, children and all you always wanted. It can happen. Don't worry, this friend won't leave your side and will give you whatever you want, no matter what you choose. But it begins with the acceptance that now, it's the time, time to be real.

The question is, how soon will you realize this and try to change?

Are you ready for it?

Your friend,
Farhan

Abeera couldn't believe someone would confront her with her life. This was embarrassing for her. But she used this as an opportunity to further work on herself and her underlying issues. She replied to him.

From: Abeera Shaikh
Date: Aug 24, 2015 7:17
Subject: Re: Exploring Abeera
To: Farhan Ahmed

Hello Farhan,

It is an immense pleasure to hear from you. So now I know my secret of confusion was not only hating myself, my background, and my family but a lot more. And while I accept all of that, I write to you.

After the roller coaster journey of my life, I am ready to accept the truth.

You have touched sensitive parts of me once again in my life, and, needless to say, they are awful.

So yes, let me tell you my story. I was born in a poor family. Gradually, when all of my siblings grew up, they worked and contributed money at home. Then after me and my younger brother moved to Dubai, we got financially much better. In childhood, my mother worked from dawn to dusk with my father, yet she faced many tortures—emotional, physical and moral—from an alcoholic, unloving, and abusive husband. She didn't respect herself and never stood up for herself.

Having witnessed this at home, I became scared of relationships from the first day. I was a neglected child like my other siblings. Nobody taught me to protect myself. The environment I grew up in was a mess. I became scared of relationships deep inside.

I helped my parents since childhood. After school, I would go to work with them until late at night. My life differed from other children's.

My father used to beat us. Not only my mother but often all of us. My childhood was full of abuse and physical torture.

Over the years, I had developed a fear-based personality. Relationships became a problem for me. For me, Men were the worst creatures on earth, and I hated them. As a result, I became a victim when I grew up and I hated myself, my family, etc.

However, I took responsibility for myself after my first breakup. It confronted a few realities I was escaping from and it forced me into an inner journey.

After the breakup, I became independent. But deep down I always felt complex. I moved from one hook-up to another. I always wanted commitment because of my fears and insecurities.

My professional life is the only area where I am comfortable. Deep down I know the office is the place where I find the most security; nobody can touch me without my permission. And now Dubai gives security to the fearful girl. But I have realized that being a workaholic and staying busy with work is only a means of escape from my buried emotions and another way to fill the void within me.

I also faced plenty of harassment and sexual abuse. My father would put me in front of others to get his work done or make life easier for himself and often send me alone with these people, who took advantage of me and sexually abused me.

Early in life, I realized that women are only a source of entertainment, pleasure, and a commodity. My father never realized that the poor little girl was suffering.

When I grew up, I thought men would be different, but to my surprise, the educated men were the same. I have struggled almost all my life with these questions: "What is sex? Is it a need? A mental sickness? Does education change men? Is there a separate sex education?"

But physiologically, it had affected me a lot.

My childhood has raised several questions:

Does education teach men to respect young girls, women at home, and women at work?

What are the responsibilities of parents? Who is to blame and who is responsible?

Marriage comes with responsibilities. Isn't it the responsibility of parents to protect their children? At least when they are young?

People often get married when they are not ready, at least in the East, or sometimes they are forced into a marriage. How would they take care of their children when they can't rightly take care of themselves?

Or are mothers supposed to be friendly enough with their daughters to share everything with them? My mother was always busy working. We were never friendly with her. And how could she have helped her daughters when she had never learned to respect herself? With whom would have I shared? My aunts and the relatives lived far away from us.

Or is it the responsibility of the teachers to teach young girls how to protect themselves?

Is there anything else our youth needs to learn other than just the education we provide to our children? Education is primary, but isn't sexual awareness a big subject?

Isn't having a joint family a better approach, so someone at home can still take care of the children, maybe our grandparents, who often become a burden for us?

The science, the economics, the statistics, physics, the geography, do we even teach our children the basic lesson of 'Love and respect for themselves?

I thank you for reminding me of this. I had just faced another reality a few months ago. Maybe to be open to accepting my childhood I had to free myself from the love I was holding for so long for my father since I had placed him on such a high pedestal.

Some of my wounds have healed, but it takes continuous work within oneself.

Oh, and I wrote a poem titled: The girl who loved herself

Enjoy.

The Healing

Staying up all nights
Searching God in the clouds
She looked insane
She laughed with everyone but cried alone
The girl who loved herself

In search of love
She had lost herself
Thought in true love you find God
But every time she failed
The girl who loved herself

She might have committed a sin
God must be angry with her
Being hurt again and again
Wondering what was happening?
The girl who loved herself

Sitting on the seashore,
She fought with herself
Walking on the terrace,
She talked to herself
The girl who loved herself

Scared with her own desires
Some clichés of her childhood
Some bad memories of the past
Some broken trust over the years
The girl who loved herself

Why am I different? What am I made for?
Why am I doing, what I am doing?
Who am I?
What do I want to achieve?
The girl who loved herself

Thanks
Abeera

Lessons we can learn from Abeera:

It's hilarious – sometimes what we do is for pleasure, or for fun, but it can have deep connotations and it's hard to predict the underlying state of a person.

If the experience of life is not brought into the conscious state, one cannot make peace.

Every experience is a chance to understand yourself more. What you accept gives you freedom.

There are layers and layers to self-acceptance. Life is a journey and every challenge you accept and work on only helps you move forward in life with grace. The choice is yours.

The respect one had longed for from their family, from men, from colleagues can only come if one has respect for themselves. And when you respect yourself you respect God.

Abeera learned about healing. Healing comes from acceptance, from accepting the situation no matter how terrible it is.

Escape from one's life only creates more trouble for oneself.

Abeera realized: That if everybody worked on themselves rather than criticizing and condemning the other, the world would be a much better place.

In life, there are no such things as coincidences: they all are interconnected and perfectly designed to fulfill the bigger purpose of life.

Lessons for parents from Abeera's life:

Child abuse is a matter of serious concern. If not taken care of, it can affect the child's entire life. Sex education, love and respect for self, should be taught by parents and even inculcated in our education system.

Parents should teach their daughters to not let anyone touch their private parts before they reach puberty, and even after puberty except with the consent of the daughter.

Parents should not allow daughters to play with boys in their absence.

Parents should give their children sex education as early as the age of 9.

Parents should teach their daughters not to shower or change their clothes in front of anyone.

Daughters shouldn't sit on anyone's lap when they are young, even if it is a close uncle.

You should return unnecessary gifts from anyone, male teachers or even family friends, or, in exceptional cases, they can give gifts to parents and not to children secretly.

Parents should not allow young girls to sit alone with a priest/cousins in a room. If they are studying together, they should do it in the lounge with everyone around.

Parents should discourage unnecessary physical interactions with any male relatives or friends.

Parents should inquire about everything that has happened during the day, asking both their sons and daughters and making sure nobody has hurt or abused them.

Chapter 8

The Forgiveness

September 2015

Abeera quit drinking. She realized dissatisfaction with life leads one to drink, overwork and sometimes get into addictive relationships.

Often, she would go accompany her friends but did not drink herself.

Abeera went to her colleague's house to congratulate him on his newborn boy. He lived in Sharjah. Going to Sharjah and not visiting her brother was something she had never imagined. Despite of everything, she still loved him.

During the last phone call Abeera had made to her brother, he gave her the cold shoulder. This time Abeera expected nothing from him. Besides, whatever Abeera was doing now was to seek the pleasure of God. She was busy building her relationship with God and enjoying each day with prayers, meditation and gratitude.

Abeera reached her brother's place. She rang the doorbell. Moiz opened the door. It surprised them all to see her. Abeera's cousins (Eman and his wife) also visited Moiz. After they all greeted each other Moiz introduced Abeera to his sister-in-law who was staying with them.

Though Abeera thought her brother would be excited to see her. But she had a devastating experience. Her brother complained, "Where were you, lost? Do you even care about your brother?" He was insulting Abeera in front of his wife and their cousins.

Abeera stayed silent. *Wasn't he enjoying himself with his family and sister-in-law? And in all these months had I ever complained that he didn't visit me or even call me? His wife had called me a few days back to inform me that Moiz had lost his job and was searching for a new job. The bank he was working with had outsourced the department. .*

Eman's husband was observing them. He told Moiz to stop complaining and have food, but his criticism was not ending, "You have time to see your friends and you were enjoying in Atlantis (The Palm, Dubai). Do you even bother to know what is happening in my life? I have lost my job. Do you know?"

Abeera ignored him again and thought, *I am here to see him. Otherwise, the family ties will break. Instead of appreciating that I was still here today to see him, he is upset with me. How many times had he called me after I had a fight with dad? Did he try to know how I managed to live on my own in all these days? Does he even realize the hurt I have gone through? What does he think I am? A machine? That I have no feelings? They can throw me out, insult me, and yet have complains with me. I can't believe it.*

They finished dinner. Abeera went to the kitchen and took off her rings to help them clean the dishes. Moiz walked in and sarcastically continued, "So

The Forgiveness

you are enjoying your freedom in Dubai. I saw your beautiful pictures on social media."

"Oh! Yes, it was a birthday gift I got from a friend. Atlantis is a lovely resort." Abeera replied.

"Oh! I see, so finally, you had time to visit your brother?" He pushed her against the wall with his leg and raised his hand on Abeera.

Abeera held his hand with her hand immediately, "Let me correct you. I am not here for you still. I am here for the pleasure of God."

He continued, "And what did you say? The house our parents live in is your house?"

"Well, it's true. By raising your voice, you can't change that fact. My God knows the truth." She replied with confidence.

His wife intervened, and, as expected, she didn't support Abeera either. She complained too.

"Sorry, you please stay out of this," Abeera told her and leaves the hand of Moiz. Assuming he won't slap her in front of his wife.

But Moiz in another second slapped Abeera.

Eman's husband rushed into the kitchen and told Moiz to stop it and took him to the room.

Abeera didn't want to get into an argument. A greater power took control over her, and, without saying a word, she put on her rings, picked up her car keys, her handbag and left.

Abeera waited for the elevator and thought, *these dominating men prove their authority by beating women. It's brutal but true. He is just like his father. No wonder it's the same pattern—a cruel father and a cruel son. I am the only victim as once my mother was. But I won't be a victim again. They can't treat me like a commodity. And why should I care? I am not dependent on these controlling men. Can he not have a conversation without proving his authority by raising his voice, or beating me up? Is it that all Eastern men are dominating, humiliating, abusive, and controlling? Or is it only my family?*

She took the elevator and walked towards her car. The cousin followed her and apologized for Moiz's behavior.

"No, don't be sorry. It is not your fault. I am so sorry that you had to see this chaos because of me and my brother. I will go now. It's better for all of us." Abeera replied calmly.

He asked Abeera, "Should I follow you home?"

Abeera replied, "No, thank you. I am fine. I will message you when I reach home, goodbye."

THE GIRL WHO LOVED HERSELF

Abeera cried on the way back home, *Thank God my cousin was there. Otherwise, I would have gotten injuries because of my brother's physical violence.*

Abeera wrote a letter to God again when she reached home:

Oh! God,
I am here again.
I know, You know everything. Not a leaf can move without your permission.
Only You are the witness of the hurt I have gone through because of these relationships.
Please save me from my relationships. Please save me.
God, I love You. I only love You.
God, I trust You. I only trust You.
Please, only You can save me.
I promise You, I will never love anyone more than You.
I will only look up to You, God, I will keep coming to You, God.
I will keep asking for forgiveness, God.
I will keep thanking You, God, for whatever you bestow upon me.
I will never complain. I will never argue.
I promise.
I surrender myself to You, God.
I submit myself to You, God.

Yours ever loving,
Abeera

Abeera also wrote a poem:

Oh! God,
My stunned eyes were blinded with your faith
What faith had taken me over?
I remember nothing but You, my beloved
All I see is You, my beloved
And I don't care what I have
As long as I have You, my beloved
Nothing matters.
I have You, and that's all that matters.

But this time the poem was for divine love. The courage shining through her was extraordinarily powerful. She had come to terms with these relationships, a girl who could now expect the worst from these relationships.

She messaged her cousin. Moiz and his wife called and apologized.

Abeera smiled and replied, "Its fine." Abeera knew their call was just a formality. But it didn't matter to her anymore. She had found a greater truth.

Abeera was doing amazingly well at work, being active on social media too, going out and watching movies, discovering new places, attending regular meditation sessions, and enjoying life with all her new friends.

For the first time, Abeera realized what true love is, "With yourself and God." What unconditional love is, "With yourself and God," and how that faith and these experiences made her so strong today. Not only from the outside but from inside.

And that is thanks to that amazing power. Without saying a word, she left when her younger brother started to abuse her. Not long ago, a personality like her would have argued back and behaved in the same way as her brother was behaving.

Abeera learned to let go. She appreciated and sought wisdom in the things she had and stopped focusing on things that were taken away from her, over which, in fact, she had no control.

Abeera went to her aunt and shared with her the state of her heart and also the last incident with her brother.

The aunt made tea for Abeera and explained to her, "Satisfaction only comes when you build your relationship with God. And to get God's love and attention you have to show love, compassion, and forgiveness to God's people. When you have love for God in your heart. You can't hate God's people."

Abeera smiled having a sip of tea, "I can understand these relationships. They have done their job. And when you taste the love of God for you, everything else becomes secondary. It brings immense peace, satisfaction and love for everything. I have never felt this before. I only practiced self-love but without God's love for you, Self-love is incomplete."

"The journey to self is a journey of challenges, a journey of trials, a journey of sorrows, and a journey of pain but an inward journey to self is a journey to God," Aunty replied and asked Abeera if she wanted to have food?

"No aunty. Thank you. What is hunger and what is thirst? My soul is enriched with God's love. And God is all I need," Abeera stood up and started the whirling dance.

The aunt brought food for Abeera and explained to her, "Indeed, all a soul needs is God's love. But a balanced life is very important. The soul is nourished only with God's love. But the physical body is a gift of God, never neglect your body. Physical fitness is as important as spiritual nourishment."

Abeera continued the whirling dance for a while. Then had food, thanked her aunt and left.

October 2015

Now was the second EID.

The night before EID, Abeera applied henna on her hands and wore her lovely black T-shirt with the message, "Love is what makes the world go round."

Beneath, Abeera was still the same loving girl. Despite the last fight with her brother, it didn't stop showering her love on him.

On the EID day, she visited them for a few hours and requested Eman to accompany her. Abeera bought a gift for the baby and spent a few hours with them. Her sister-in-law ordered pizza for her. They enjoyed food together but they were depressed because of Moiz no longer having a job. Abeera could understand but she couldn't help much. She sent Moiz's resume to a few friends to help him find a job.

The next day, their cousin, Eman called Abeera to invite her for the EID holidays, as they all wanted to travel to Abu Dhabi with Abeera.

For the first time in life, Abeera joined them as a formality. Abeera felt scared deep inside that her brother might strike up a conversation again and hit her. Even though they all were together Abeera enjoyed with the children, with the baby, her cousins, and the music, and avoided interactions with her brother.

They all had the same tastes for music, and even if Moiz and his wife weren't talking to her, she enjoyed listening to music together.

Abeera felt more comfortable with cousins than her own loved ones. Sometimes you feel more comfortable with relatives than your own family.

They left for their homes. The trip ended well. Abeera didn't expect that. No arguments, no violence, no criticism.

At least they spent a few hours together without messing up.

December 2015

Another two months passed enjoying Dubai life.

Abeera was having coffee with a friend. Her phone rang. She looked at the phone. It was her father's call from Pakistan. He was crying and requested Abeera to visit Pakistan. Abeera said nothing and booked the flight to Lahore for the UAE National day holidays.

The Forgiveness

That's the thing with pain. When you go through pain in your life, you can't see anyone in pain. Abeera thought.

Abeera ditched all the lovely plans she had made with her friends. The National Day celebrations had started and after a busy day at work, Abeera reached home, changed, and took a cab to the airport.

At the airport, she called Amir and told him she was leaving for Lahore as her father had called her. It surprised Amir. He angrily replied, "Are you in your senses? What does he want now? So now he is missing his daughter. He never wanted a daughter. He wanted a commodity, a slave to his commands. Can you not see that? For all these months he had never found out if you were alive, he didn't want to talk and had not kept in contact. You had no choice. Does he realize how hurt you were because of his behavior?"

Abeera stayed quiet for a while thinking, *had he changed his mind? What could I possibly have done? If I wanted to do something only for myself, I would have bought something for myself and never mentioned it to him, but I wanted to do something for them.*

Amir was waiting on the phone, "Hello, I am talking to you. Are you there?"

"Yes, I am here. My father is upset is all I know. He needs me." Abeera replied.

"Abeera stop being stupid. He has only called you because his son has lost his job. He hasn't called you from his heart and love. Do you think he regretted what he did? He wants to use you again. Please don't allow him to do that."

Abeera was silent again, *in the past, when I used to cry in the middle of the night, I would call dad and often hug my brother. During all these months, did they ever think once about what I would do? I was so scared for so many nights. I felt I would die with the witch that was coming in my dreams again and again.*

"Abeera, please say something, I am worried about you." Amir was waiting on the phone again.

Abeera replied, "Don't worry, I have God with me. I am not alone. God is with me. God will protect me."

Amir couldn't understand, "Abeera please don't do this to yourself. These people are not trustworthy. Can you not see that?"

Abeera replied, "How much can they use me?"

"It is not that. They are not concerned about you." Amir replied.

"What difference would a few dirhams make?" Abeera said.

"Abeera please try to understand, It's not about money—the injustice, the insincerity, the humiliation, and the domination. You don't deserve this."

"You are right Amir. But what more can happen? I didn't die in these last few months. I will be fine. God is with me I told you. They are my family. They are not enemies. They are humans. And humans make mistakes."

"Abeera you are so innocent you are allowing them to use you and hurt you again. Please tell your father you are all right without him, and you don't need him nor the family."

"You are right Amir. You have rightly said. I don't need them. In fact, I need no one. I only need God. And I am doing all this for God. And when you do things for God, you don't have to worry. I want to please God. All my life I have done nothing for God. I want God to give attention to me. I want God to look at me and tell me He is with me. Please let me go."

Amir was worried about her, "Take care. I don't understand you. Hope everything goes well with you. Stay in touch."

"I will be fine. Don't worry. See you soon." Abeera replied and put the phone down.

Abeera landed. Her parents picked her up from the airport. Abeera gave her passport to her mother when they reached home and told her, "Mom, please, if anything goes wrong, just hand over my passport. I will go back. I am not here to fight with anyone."

Abeera's mother had never seen her so weak and fearful. All her life she had seen Abeera as a courageous, strong, and fearless person. Abeera's sister looked at her in surprise.

All night the ladies gossiped, and Abeera kept listening quietly. Abeera had no resistance, *how do you expect someone to resist when there is nothing outside to battle with?*

A new chapter of her life had been revealed to her. The only relationship that mattered now to her was her relationship with God.

The next morning, Abeera spoke to her parents. But that could not change the pain and suffering she had experienced during the lonely dark nights. Their betrayal had changed her life. But they were still the same, trying to control her, possess her, and wrong here.

Abeera apologized and told them, "I have no grudge against anyone. I let you decide whatever you want to do with this house. Even though practically, it will be unfair to me. I am only here to ask for forgiveness and ease your pain. I wanted to come earlier, but I had no courage since dad was angry with me. This property is not mine. If you have the love for God in your heart, you don't calculate the losses and the profits. Nothing is mine. Everything is of God, and to God, we all shall return."

The Forgiveness

That night Abeera wrote a poem:

I remember all the troubles you have caused me
I haven't forgotten a single bit
The heartaches, the sadness, the loneliness
You never loved me, nor trusted me
But now I cannot love you
More than myself, more than my God.

Don't find the love you saw once in my eyes.
I can never come back
And come back where, in this family of madness?
Don't ask me to come back
My heart doesn't long for you anymore
My heart doesn't want those who
Shattered, abandoned, tarnished me

And now I cannot love you
More than myself, more than my God.

The next day, Abeera took her father to the doctor for his regular check-up. Abeera's father congratulated her on her new car.

Abeera replied, "Thank you. A friend of mine helped me buy it. Times pass."

Abeera's mom was so happy to see her. She had been meditating and praying for her and her father.

Before returning to Dubai, Abeera was crying in the room. Abeera's father came and took her to his room, hugged her, and asked her that she should get married now, "A husband gives security to his wife." Abeera smiled and replied, "No one and nothing can give you security, the relationships, the belongings or money. The security only comes from God."

After Abeera returned to Dubai, she went to see her aunt. She shared the story of what happened in Pakistan and told her, "I forgave my family from the core of my heart. I am glad I clarified my position."

The aunt was happy for Abeera and explained to her, "We all have attributes of God. Forgiveness is an attribute of God. When you forgive others, God forgives you." she continued, "You are very courageous. Your capacity to love and forgive is astonishing. Sometimes in life, you have to sacrifice your relationships to make room for God's love for you. You have to sacrifice your dear ones and your worldly desires."

She also quoted the spiritual stage in Islam, "What you have experienced is the false attachment to the material realm and you could transcend notions of self. In Islam the sacrifice demanded is one's personal willingness to submit their will to the will of God."

Abeera asked her aunt, "I want to know what God's desire is for me. I now want to do what God expects from me. What God has chosen for me? How do I know?"

She replied, "God's desire lies in the desire of your heart. Seek within."

"Thank you, aunty, but now my only desire is the desire of God. I need nothing and no one."

Abeera's aunt informed her that she was now moving back to Pakistan soon. Abeera thanked her aunt for being with her for all this time. Abeera told her, "I will miss your company but now I have God with me, I can never be alone."

Lessons we can learn from Abeera

When you stop pleasing people and instead please God, we experience God's presence.

To experience God, one has to let go, let go of all the logic of the mind and follow their heart.

All relationships are just a 'means' to God. Unless God wants it from us, or for us, we can do nothing.

Every adversity, every calamity, every misery is nothing but an opportunity to connect to God, If you keep turning to God, He will never leave you alone.

There is a purpose for every relationship in your life.

If God is with you, nothing matters and nothing could be more beautiful than a story that leads you to God.

No matter how difficult and threatening life becomes, God can do miracles, have faith.

Abeera learned to show forgiveness to those who never accept their mistakes.

Powerful is not somebody who fights back. Powerful is somebody who fights with himself. All battles are within.

Chapter 9

The Transcending of Hurt

THE GIRL WHO LOVED HERSELF

January 2016

Abeera's brother had now moved to Lahore. The bank gave him a few months of visa to find a job but he couldn't find one and eventually had to leave Dubai.

Abeera had changed completely, from late night partying to meditation gatherings; from traveling for fun to attend spiritual retreats; from socializing to real connections; from solitude to companionship; from being emotional to awareness; from being a victim to being a creator. Her lifestyle changed.

In the evenings, she would meditate, and she had stopped going out with her friends. Her friends and colleagues became worried about her; some of them would make fun of her. But she was so busy with her new discoveries, learnings, and writings that nothing was more appealing to her.

On the weekends she would go to Imran's house for meditation.

And then came the time of people asking for her forgiveness.

First, one was Kamal, he had broken her heart the last time she had met him.

Without calling, he came directly to her door, rang the bell, but she didn't open it. He stayed there for close to one hour, but she stood firm and did not let him in.

The following morning, he called her and professed, "I wanted to apologize to you for my behavior the last time we met, so I came over to your place yesterday."

She thanked him for the call and replied, "I like your honesty. May God bless you. God likes honesty and people who accept their mistakes."

Then the second case.

Another call she received was from Samar:

He told her, "I have called only to apologize you for not staying in touch with you."

Abeera replied, "I am sorry for my rude behavior as well."

"I have really enjoyed our conversations and sometimes I missed you." He told her, feeling guilty.

Abeera was very confused, for a long time she waited for his calls and message, "I missed you too."

"I have started a business in Dubai and moved here recently." And continued his sentence, "Would you meet me?"

Abeera agreed to meet him and said thank you for the call.

And then the third:

The Transcending of Hurt

The next day, an old uncle who had abused her when she was 17 years old, was in Dubai for a business meeting. He called Abeera to meet up. She was very scared to meet him, but this time she had drawn strong boundaries for herself and for him. She met him at the reception area of the hotel lobby.

When she was young, she had immensely admired this uncle. To her surprise, he apologized to her for his behavior and explained to her, "We men can be very weak sometimes and end up doing things we should not, especially when there is a girl we admire."

She was not only glad but equally surprised at what was happening and how suddenly these men were apologizing to her.

For the first time in life, Abeera felt totally secure, completely free, and contented.

Abeera had completely surrendered to God and His will for her. She had no grudges against anyone.

She wrote a poem titled: "I see you God."

The waves of the water
The smiling lilies
The silent trees
The birds chirping
Is it You, is it You?

My soul thirsts for You
My heart cries for You
I search for me and I see You
I search for You and I see me
Is it You, is it You?

Where am I? Who am I?
My body is intoxicated in Your love
Your desire is my desire
Is it You? Is it me or is it, love!
I love You and I love myself!

Abeera was now building her relationship with God through everything. Nature, the animals, the weather, herself and etc. All she thought of was God,

THE GIRL WHO LOVED HERSELF

"God is everywhere, and God is the center of everything."

February 2016

Abeera went to Oman to attend a spiritual retreat for a few days.

There she met Sultan, he was much older than her, almost her father's age. He was married and had daughters of Abeera's age. Abeera became friends with him.

The Oman retreat was amazing. It comprised only a few people, they all were very loving and caring, just like Abeera's meditation friends in Dubai.

Abeera stayed with a family. She felt so at peace and was once again amazed to have met some nice people in life.

She wished she could have spent more days as it was just a three-day retreat.

After she returned to Dubai, Abeera explained to her friends about her meditation practices and wrote many notes on self-love and how she had now become a lover of life and a lover of reality. Some of her friends understood her and admired her; others thought she had gone crazy. But that was nothing for her to worry about; she was completely satisfied with herself at last.

Abeera realized that in life, you can't make everyone happy. When she was outgoing, people criticized her, and now when she has turned into a home-loving and spiritual person, people still had issues.

Whatsoever she did now, she needed no praise outside of herself.

All her sadness of life had transcended. She could feel different, new and vibrant, full and complete, enthusiastic and bewildered.

Abeera was enjoying and writing poems:

As clear as a mirror, the joy of silence
As quiet, as peaceful, the pleasure the morning brings with it
Me and my loneliness and the beautiful sunrise view
The view of the pool, the silence of the morning
What a beautiful view, every part of my body seems alive

Lovely water and me, dancing, playing, smiling
The dark silent night, my body dances
The warmth of the water, my heart dances,
The moon smiling with me, the stars shining
The moon's reflection in the water, pure delight,
Pure love, pure nature and pure life
Angels are surrounding me

The Transcending of Hurt

Sun shining over the dunes
The grass growing on the plains
Children playing all around
A quite long walk, look at the birds chirping,
Was she talking to me? What did she say?
Her voice so soft, like the freshness of the breeze

After the retreat Abeera would talk to Sultan regularly, who listened to her stories every evening.

One day, while browsing through a website on one of the Sufi pages, she came across the details of a Malaysian retreat. It was also a three-day retreat in Langkawi.

Abeera got overly excited as she had really enjoyed the retreat in Oman the last time.

Now she wanted to travel with a purpose; to travel for spiritual growth.

She asked Sultan if he would accompany her so they both could travel together and attend the retreat. Sultan agreed, and they booked the tickets together.

May 2016

Abeera was enjoying her 'newfound transformed self' in Dubai.

In the last few months, she would often sit in the balcony and wonder how beautiful her life had become.

After a few days Abeera travelled and met Sultan in the transit at Doha Airport.

Abeera asked Sultan, "What is a success for you?"

Sultan replied, "I am successful. I have a well-paid job, a big house and a very loving family."

Abeera replied, "Well! You are blessed."

"But that is not the answer I have. Most people think success is just what you described. Real success for me is the inner success followed by the outer success. Not the other way round. The car, the house, the job and everything else will follow."

The answer of Abeera surprised Sultan. He sometimes not believed Abeera could talk like this.

They landed at the airport in Kuala Lumpur. Abeera had developed some intuitive abilities which were much stronger than before. When they landed, she took Sultan's phone and wrote the following lines on social media:

THE GIRL WHO LOVED HERSELF

Today, I will know the desire of God
In my heart, I know
O my God, thank You
O my God, thank You

Sultan, for the first time, told Abeera, "Now I trust that you are a writer!" Abeera laughed.

Over the past year, Abeera had connected to her inner self. Writing had really helped her to understand things she couldn't otherwise, and she could also interpret the meanings of dreams, signs, and coincidences.

When they came out of the airport, it was raining. Abeera enjoyed the rain. Rain had always mesmerized her. She wrote, "Somewhere something is happening on this planet for me. I am ignorant but certainly, my heart knows."

However, she still didn't know this trip to Malaysia would change her life forever. The dream she had long awaited was now coming true. God had sent a gift for her. God had answered her prayers.

But her desire was to know the desire of God.

They organized the retreat beautifully in Langkawi with two big villas to accommodate 40-50 people. People gathered in Kuala Lumpur in the morning at 11:00 am. Then they took a bus to Langkawi.

This was the beginning of one of the most holidays in Malaysia and the roads were jammed. Abeera made some new friends on the bus, introduced herself, listened to spiritual stories and shared her spiritual experiences. When they reached Langkawi, they said their afternoon prayers, followed by lunch.

After lunch, Abeera rushed to her room and slept. She shared the room with a lady from Pakistan who she eventually became friends with.

After a few hours, Abeera came down for the evening tea, and, while waiting to be served, a very handsome man entered and sat at the opposite table. Abeera gazed at him, trying hard to resist. He looked from the west. He was tall and gorgeously attractive. Abeera never had friends from the West. The last time she got attracted to someone from the West was in a bar she and her friend would go to. She always thought Westerners were open-minded and had a soft corner for them.

Abeera turned around a few times and kept gazing at him. After a few times, she forced herself to stop and reminded herself to not fall into the repeated trap with men she had experienced all her life. But he was so damn attractive! She did not know Westerners also attend the retreat. Nonetheless, she didn't think about that moment again during the retreat.

The next morning, she woke up and left the bed in her favorite PJs for early morning prayers. PJs had always been her favorite attire, easy, and comfortable to wear. After the prayers and group meditation, she walked along the coast with Sultan. It was beautiful and serene.

They came back from the walk and had breakfast. After breakfast Sultan introduced her to the Westerner she gazed at even though she had mentioned nothing to him.

"This is Abeera, also a banker from Dubai."

And then Sultan introduced him, "This is Antoine. He works for a bank in London. He is a reverted Muslim, and, yes, he is French. You would not have guessed?"

Abeera replied, "Interesting, yes. I have no French friends."

She excitedly tried to engage in a conversation with Antoine. "So, Antoine, how did you convert?"

Antoine replied casually, "Oh! That's a long story."

"Damn, he is so cold," Abeera thought inside, but she didn't care.

That was the only interaction she had with him.

The three-day retreat ended. Now the meditation group had to travel back to Kuala Lumpur. Most of the people had already left for their hometowns. The end of the retreat and being away from her new friends made her extremely sad. The three days passed very quickly. Every night Abeera and her close friends would spend a few hours after dinner together in the lobby and enjoy the moments full of laughter. Abeera felt she was back in her teens.

In the afternoon, they left for Kuala Lumpur. Some people still had time before catching their flights, so they stayed at a friend's place in Kuala Lumpur for the evening.

In the afternoon, a small group went downtown and visited Petronas Towers. When they reached outside the Petronas Towers, Sultan turned back as he felt sick and didn't join them. Abeera got upset with him as all other people left were new and she did not know them. Then they took the train and Abeera and Antoine were the first ones to board it. Abeera initiated a dialogue with Antoine.

"So which department do you work for?"

Antoine replied, "Well! I do many things, but basically, I am in investment banking. And you?"

"Well, me too I do many things, but basically I am a relationship manager in retail banking."

"Ah! Show me the money."

"Yes, my job is to open accounts and ask customers to deposit money. So, how long have you been in London?" She continued.

"I moved to London in 2006. It is 10 years now. And you?"

"I moved to Dubai in 2012. It is four years now."

"You look young. How long have you been in the Sufi group?" He asked.

"Yes, I am young. I had known the group for a few years but I started regularly meditation a few months ago."

Abeera thought to herself, *how do I share with what I have gone through and why I couldn't meditate*?

"Hmm, did someone recommend the group to you?"

"No. It's funny. Would you believe Me, I Google and came across their page? I didn't know if it was a Sufi group. I wanted peace." She laughed.

"That's interesting. I can understand."

It was time to get off the train.

Abeera continued talking.

A friend gave coins for the train to Abeera and Antoine.

Abeera told Antoine, "In Dubai we use train cards."

"Yes, even in London, look." He showed her the tube card from his wallet.

"That reminds me, I lost my card somewhere."

"How?"

"I might have dropped it somewhere or it might be in my room. I will try to find it when I go back." She said.

"How long are you here in Kuala Lumpur?"

"I love traveling. I will stay here for another two days. And you?"

"Well, I am flying out tonight. I have to go to work tomorrow."

"And guess what, my weekend is off and I am off on 5th May. It is a public holiday in Dubai, so a long weekend."

"Lucky you."

People were ordering food. They asked Abeera and Antoine their preferred food.

Antoine replied, "I am relaxed, anything."

Abeera also replied, "I am relaxed, too."

All of their friends were secretly laughing, seeing Abeera and Antoine so busy talking.

"This is my second retreat. I attended one before in Oman. This one is relatively big." Abeera told Antoine.

"In London, we have a big group."

"Really? In Dubai, we are just a few people who meet, around six! It's a tiny group."

Antoine continued, "I will get food for myself. Do you want something else?"

"No, thanks, my friend will bring the nasi paprika, the Malaysian food for me." She replied.

"Ok, good."

Abeera was looking beautiful, in her Beryline colored T-shirt, multi-colored loose trousers, a red scarf, and a lovely light brown bag.

She was enjoying the view of the fountain. Soon her friend came with the food. She thanked him.

And then Antoine came with his food. He sat right across Abeera. They talked again.

"So, do you watch movies?" Abeera asked.

"Yes."

"Do you watch movies?" He asked.

"Yes, I watch action movies, sometimes."

"Oh, and what are your hobbies?"

"Reading, writing, traveling, and meditating," Abeera laughed inside, it reminded her the trip to Nepal.

"And you?"

"As same as you," and he asked, "Do you like your food or you want something else?"

"No, no I am fine, thank you."

Soon after some friends finished lunch. They were heading to the bookstore. Abeera wanted to buy books for herself. She excused herself and followed the other friends.

She went to the bookshop and picked up a few books. While she was in the queue to pay for the books, Antoine came up right beside her and asked, "Which books did you buy? Can I see?"

She showed the books to him.

They left the store together and continued talking.

"These books relate to loving yourself," Abeera said.

"Love yourself, what? That sounds selfish," he replied.

"Ah! I am not surprised. Many of my friends think like that, but no, it means, 'I don't overlook or compromise myself, as I love myself enough.' For example, someone hurts you emotionally and you confront them, or you break up with someone who is very abusive or critical of you. When you put yourself above everyone else and make yourself a priority and become responsible for yourself, 'to own yourself' means you love yourself. It's simple. We negate ourselves in

THE GIRL WHO LOVED HERSELF

small ways. I have been learning this for the last few years."

"That's interesting. I think it is self-obsession. No, I am just kidding," he continued, "Actually I had a friend who always said I love myself but I felt she was closed, that is why I feel love yourself is a selfish concept. But I liked the way you explained."

"I am not surprised. But if you know the real meaning of 'love yourself', then you can better understand. It is very interesting but it can be very tricky; be careful. It's like—I want to say I am not dependent on anyone for my happiness, but the underlying reasons could be many. One is for selfish reasons where one can be defensive knowingly or unknowingly. The other is a state when one has learned to trust in themselves and God."

"But I didn't mean to upset you," he said.

Abeera laughed, "Don't worry. I am not upset."

"Can I offer you a drink?" Antoine asked.

"Sure."

"Which juice do you want?"

"The mixed fruit juice."

"Ok." Antoine looked for a table, and they both sat down to drink.

"So, what is your view on marriage?"

Abeera laughed again.

"Why do you laugh?"

"You remind me of a guy I met last year. Someone recommended him for marriage. He was weird. He had a checklist of questions, and you know, the worst was when he said, 'I want a partner who can share the finances with me, as life is expensive and I want to get my sister and my brother married.' It was ridiculous.

"I feel a few responsibilities are for men and only men, no matter what. Anyway. But sorry, you have touched on a subject which I have done research on LOL. Pardon me. If I may say so, marriage looks like a trade."

"I understand what you say, but the West is more open to sharing the expenses and everything equally. But why would you say marriage is a trade?"

"Because it all boils down to, if you fulfill my needs, I will fulfill yours. It's all about need- fulfillment."

"Ah! And what about love?" Antoine was curious.

"'Love' is a word people use instead of saying, 'I scratch your back, you scratch mine.'"

"That's so crude. I am surprised someone from an Eastern background thinks like this. But marriage provides one with security, and, as you say, need-fulfillment."

"That's a truth of many people. In truth, marriage is a 'means', as are many things in life: a 'means' to fulfill your purpose of life."

Antoine replied, "I really need to follow you on this."

Anyway, she continued her story of the guy she was introduced to, "He asked me stupid questions like, 'how many gifts do you prefer in a year?' And that he was ready to clean, cook, etc. and only wanted me to share the finances. That is a business, a deal, a partnership based on responsibilities and sharing. That is not marriage."

"Ok, but what is so wrong with sharing responsibilities?" Antoine asked.

"Nothing, but the foundation of a relationship should be something deeper. And maybe I am old-fashioned, as some of my friends say. I believe finances are entirely a man's responsibility. What I earn or don't earn should not mean he should give up on his responsibilities."

"That is understandable, some women think like this, but not all," Antoine replied.

She continued the story, "But, he was funny. I shared this experience with a few friends and it did not surprise them. These days, with women being independent, everything has changed. In the name of freedom, women are being used by men without even realizing it. But it's good he was upfront. Usually, men are not so vocal about that in the East—well, at least where I come from. Men use and manipulate women but never mention that."

Abeera thought, *who can better know this than me? Sh*e changed the topic quickly.

"Anyway, how did you revert?" She inquired.

"My reverting to Islam has been a long journey. My friend introduced me to the group. I had the same impression of Islam being a conservative and strict religion. People view Islam as a 'foreign culture,' but if you separate the core belief from the cultural aspects, you're left with a beautiful belief true for everyone. 'There is one God and Mohammed (May peace be upon him) is his Prophet.' In Islam, I discovered that it fitted with my image of God. I was a Christian before I reverted to Islam. And Jesus is what it all comes down to. I don't believe Jesus is the son of God."

Antoine paused and took a sip of his juice and continued, "Islam is a religion of peace, and, the media propaganda which highlights Muslims for non-Islamic values has undermined the uniqueness of the religion. Many people are reverting from the West. They understand Islam and not the cultural aspects of Muslims."

"May God bless you, Antoine."

Three hours passed quickly. They also took pictures with their friends and went back to their friends place to meditate.

After meditation, Antoine had to leave and could only wave to Abeera to say goodbye, along with other friends.

Later in the evening, Abeera told Sultan about the lovely conversation with Antoine and how all her friends had congratulated Abeera. The mindsets of these friends didn't surprise her.

"It's funny," she said, "Just because I had a few conversations with Antoine meant there is something between us."

Sultan was happy to hear Abeera and Antoine could speak for so long. He admired her and Antoine. He thought if they married, they would be a lovely couple. He tried to convince Abeera that she should get serious with her life and get married to Antoine. Abeera laughed. She hated lectures as always. Who knew her struggles to get over her dream of getting married? Yet Sultan didn't stop. He gave her Antoine's email address and asked her to write to him.

Soon, she wrote to Antoine.

From: Abeera Shaikh
Date: May 4, 2016 2:39
Subject: Hello
To: Antoine Paris

>Hello,
>Hope you reached home safe and everything went well!
>
>Sultan gave me your email address.
>Just wanted to say thanks for the lovely chat yesterday.

Thanks,
Abeera

From: Antoine Paris
Date: May 4, 2016 10:53
Subject: Re: Hello
To: Abeera Shaikh

>Hello,
>Back in London. It is sunny but cold. But back home.
>Thanks for the email. I enjoyed our conversations, especially as it was a 2-way discussion.

I learned it is important to consider others' points of view and not just try to impose one's views on others.

But I still believe we make our lives harder than necessary, as we try to find the perfect environment for ourselves, and that dilutes our happiness more than anything else.

Hope to see you soon in London (give me a shout when you get time), in Dubai or somewhere else in the world.

Hope you enjoy your last 2 days in Kuala Lumpur!
Antoine

Abeera was having coffee with Sultan in Kuala Lumpur when Antoine sent his reply. Sultan was more excited than she was. He read the email before she read it herself!

She wrote a reply to Antoine and explained to him about self-love as her aunt had explained to her.

From: Abeera Shaikh
Date: May 5, 2016 12:33
Subject: Re: Re: Hello
To: Antoine Paris

Hello,
Thank you for your email.

It's too cold in London, and we in Dubai can't live without air conditioners; it's hot most of the year.

Yes, nothing is perfect in life.

We have everything within ourselves and that's when we connect to ourselves. Real love is Self-love. Love for self and love for God is interchangeable. Love yourself and you love God. Respect yourself and you respect God. The source of joy, the source of love and the source of life is only that intimate connection with yourself and God. Though God is everywhere and nothing exists outside God but to experience God one has to go within, contemplate and reflect. Through true love for self, you can experience God's presence.

Many of my friends argue about other relationships in life. Parents, siblings, friends, etc. Everyone is equal in the eyes of God and every relationship has its own responsibility. There is nothing more important than oneself I believe. If we are true to ourselves, we are true to God. When we honor ourselves, we honor God.

I would like to see you again too, maybe in London, but it depends on the

visa. Maybe we can plan a trip somewhere else. What do you say?
    I am going back to Dubai now. I guess I am getting old and a Sufi now (LOL).
    Take care, speak to you soon.
Abeera

From: Antoine Paris
Date: May 7, 2016 11:10
Subject: Day-to-day talk
To: Abeera Shaikh

    Hello Abeera,
    Ah, the Sufi impact on our day-to-day lives. What excited me before has lost most of its appeal.
    I had dinner with a friend yesterday. The ambiance was heavy, with drunk people and women with mini-skirts.
    I understand what you said about self-love. There are many ways to reach God. God is found in the mosque, in the church, in nature, in a child, in sadness, in happiness etc. but I have read a few poets who talk about self and God.
You are right, trust in God is essential.
    It will be my pleasure to meet you again.
    Is there a retreat in Dubai?
    Hope you have a safe trip back to your marvelous Dubai!
Take care
Antoine

From: Abeera Shaikh
Date: May 8, 2016 16:13
Subject: Re: Day-to-day talk
To: Antoine Paris

Thanks for your email!
Hope you are enjoying your weekend.
Yes, I am back in Dubai, back to work, love Dubai, love work, too hot though.
Retreat in Dubai, no.
    Are you not on social media? I searched for you but could not find you. I wonder how people lived in the olden days, without the social media, how they survived without being connected all the time. Now millions of people are online at the same time. I love technology and the way it has progressed over the years.

But we'd better be careful – it's also true that with the internet and its availability, people have the tendency to lose real connections.
Take care
Abeera

    Abeera returned to Dubai and told her friends about her trip and how she felt connected to this French guy, Antoine.
After a few days, Antoine sent her an email again.

From: Antoine Paris
Date: May 20, 2016 2:00
Subject: The rush
To: Abeera Shaikh

    Hello,
    The rush has started again. Feels like a stretch every day. Running around, and little time to breathe.
    I will write to you this weekend.
    In the meantime, enjoy your Friday.
Take care
Antoine

From: Abeera Shaikh
Date: May 23, 2016 15:45
Subject: Re: The rush
To: Antoine Paris

Hello,
    Ah! Banking is a busy and a hectic job. I can understand.
    I think if we can travel somewhere these EID holidays in July, EID should fall on the 6th or 7th July. Are you free?
    Hope you have a nice day!
Abeera

From: Antoine Paris
Date: May 26, 2016 10:38
Subject: Traveling
To: Abeera Shaikh

THE GIRL WHO LOVED HERSELF

Hello,

 Traveling is a good idea. I have not planned long holidays for the summer and I want to take a break. Do you have any place in mind? Italy is nice, though hot in the summer, but not as hot as Dubai, I am sure. Rome is good. What do you suggest? Do you need a visa?

 And Ramadan is on our doorstep. Amazing, no? I was afraid a few weeks ago, and now I am looking forward to it. I drink coffee every day, so the first few days of fasting will be detox mode, and I forecast a few headaches.
Enjoy your day!
Antoine

From: Abeera Shaikh
Date: Jun 1, 2016 14:07
Subject: Re: Traveling
To: Antoine Paris

Hello,

 Indeed! Italy is amazing, but I need a visa for most parts of the world. But, I'm sorry, I don't want to go to Europe for now, although I love it. However, we can go to many other places, like Morocco, Turkey, Thailand, Africa, and Indonesia. What do you say?

 And yes, I am looking forward to Ramadan too. The best part is the late-night prayers. I love them.

 I hope you have fewer headaches. Good luck and Ramadan Kareem (Wishing the holy month) in advance.
Abeera

 Abeera didn't tell Antoine that her biggest dream was traveling to Europe with her husband, especially for her honeymoon, a dream she had given up.

From: Antoine Paris
Date: Jun 5, 2016 10:34
Subject: Traveling Dates
To: Abeera Shaikh

Hello,

 I was expecting it would be a problem to get the visa.
 It is not clear when I can take holidays in July. That is why I took a few days

to reply to you regarding dates, could you go from Friday to Sunday or Monday? Just investigating our options.

And regarding destinations, they all look super attractive. Would Istanbul also interest you?

I am not active on social media. I am not a social person, though I have been more active in connecting with people through different channels over the past couple of months than before, it takes a lot of energy and time. Though I don't deny there are benefits. I am getting more into it. And are you still active on social media? Or are you busy with Ramadan preparations?

Have a blessed Ramadan.
Antoine

From: Abeera Shaikh
Date: Jun 7, 2016 11:01
Subject: Re: Traveling Dates
To: Antoine Paris

Hello,

A few days ago I moved to my new apartment, which is a mess right now and keeps me busy. I have been so busy with the move, and it is so hectic. I have got a fever.

Yesterday was the first day of Ramadan. I felt exhausted. How about you?

Social media, I am always active (LOL). It's my passion to write. I made a blog which I actively write on. People have different views on social media these days. But I think *"One should find meaning for themselves in every relationship. The relationship to social media as well."*

EID should fall on 6 or 7 July, depending on the moon. The following Friday and Saturday are my off days. We can spend a long weekend together if we travel. Istanbul, I love it. I have been there 3 years ago, but that's fine. We can still go again.

Take care
Abeera

From: Antoine Paris
Date: Jun 13, 2016 1:43
Subject: Ramadan
To: Abeera Shaikh

THE GIRL WHO LOVED HERSELF

Hello,

Already 1 week of Ramadan is behind us and getting into the 2nd week. It has been busy at work. The first 2 days of Ramadan felt intense and difficult. I always need a few days to settle in. With such short nights here in the UK, Ramadan gets challenging and busy. I went for prayers last night and today. There is a mosque just 5 minutes' walk from my place, very convenient. And you? Did you find a mosque nearby?

Do you like your new place? Do you live alone? Or with friends? Why did you move? Sorry if my questions are too personal.

A few days out would be super nice. I am still working on that. If it does not work, we can schedule a long weekend later in the summer. Let us see.

Are your working hours different during Ramadan?

And what do you write? Your favorite "love yourself"?

Have a blessed 2nd week of Ramadan.

Antoine

From: Abeera Shaikh
Date: Jun 14, 2016 11:32
Subject: Re: Ramadan
To: Antoine Paris

Hello,

The other day while I was writing to you, one of my friends called me old-fashioned (LOL).

My writings relate to self, spirituality, relationships and God.

I love my new apartment. About your question, it was a dream to live in this community. I loved it. And now I moved into this apartment. It's kind of resort, with a big pool, a barbeque area, a kids' play area, a garden, a gym, a Jacuzzi, covered parking in the basement and it is very secure, even though Dubai itself is very secure.

I don't mind your questions. Don't worry. Yes, I live alone since 2014. Before I lived with my brother.

Ramadans are superb here. Dubai boasts majestic and beautiful mosques and most of the mosques have prayer areas for women. Yes, I found a mosque close to my new place, just 5 minutes' walk.

Ramadan timings are 2 hours less. We get overloaded with work. The same amount of work but less time.

Do you meditate daily? Do you live alone? If it's ok to ask?

Enjoy Ramadan and remember me in your prayers.
Abeera

From: Antoine Paris
Date: Jun 20, 2016 8:22
Subject: Short Message
To: Abeera Shaikh

Hello,

Just a quick note to tell you it has been hectic over the past week.

I will email you tomorrow. I am traveling to Paris for a client meeting and I should have time to write in the Eurostar on my way back.

I hope all goes well on your end. Already half of Ramadan is behind us.

And yes, I meditate daily. Without it, my life seems incomplete.

In the West, we usually live on our own. There is no joint family system like East. West is more focused on individuality.

Wish you light!
Antoine

From: Antoine Paris
Date: Jun 23, 2016 3:14
Subject: A big email
To: Abeera Shaikh

Hello,

Intense is the word. It is too intense. 2 days ago on my way back to London in the Eurostar; I slept all the way. I came back home at 8:30 pm I did my prayers and then waited for 9:25 pm but fell asleep and woke up at midnight. Had to push hard to stand up and do all that I needed: cook, pray, and eat. The last 10 days are coming soon. I need to prepare myself to do more prayers and get the blessings of Ramadan.

I enjoy our communication. It's my pleasure we are in touch after the Malaysian retreat. Again, staying in contact with people has never been my forte. I am getting better at it though. There is a balance between being a lone wolf and an online social addict.

I don't think the medium is old-fashioned. Writing a letter forces you to think. It can provide an edge to the communication and increase the overall quality of the communication and for people to better know each other. Do you agree?

Yes, I live alone and it is a big test for me. After reverting to Islam I am no Mr. Perfect, but seriously, I feel much more grounded. I appreciate and accept my life where I come from and where I am heading to.

Tonight, I will go home early and try to go to bed at 11:30 pm and wake up at 2:00 am for the morning breakfast 'Sehri' for fasting.

Are you settled in your new place? It always takes time. Sometimes it may take a few months to get all in order.

And last but not least, yes, it would be great to see each other soon. I might have a few days after EID. So let us work on that.

Please share your recent writings!

Have blessed last days of Ramadan.

Antoine

From: Abeera Shaikh
Date: Jun 24, 2016 19:43
Subject: Re: A big email
To: Antoine Paris

Hello,

Interesting.

"Letter," yes, I agree. In writing, you get time to collect your thoughts and put them on paper.

I laughed when I read, "lone wolf." I have loved solitude for a long time. My friends think I am crazy because I can live alone and enjoy it. But 'solitude is bliss'. The first thing is peace with yourself rest everything follows in its own way and its own time.

Mr. Perfect (LOL). Good luck. You might be your other half's Mr. Perfect (LOL).

Yes, the apartment will take time, if I don't procrastinate.

We can decide the dates to meet, for sure.

Good luck for your prayers and enjoy Ramadan.

Take care.

And here is the note I recently wrote: "Spirituality and relationships." This is one of the biggest lessons I have learned in life.

Relationships are the most challenging subject in today's life. The number of divorces is increasing day by day. Couples quickly fall out of love. Parents are not happy with their children and sometimes children are not happy with their parents. Our technologies and science have succeeded. Even the field of medicine, and now the new artificial intelligence, are all commendable, but in relationships, we are still where we used to be decades ago: insecure, jealous, possessive, etc. Why do relationships bring hurt?

Relationships hurt and become problematic because we don't understand the basic reasons of a relationship and we haven't used relationships for their real purpose, which goes for all relationships, whether they are romantic or other relationships. We have relationships with everything around us, relationships with the weather, the neighbors, this moment, life, money, self, etc.

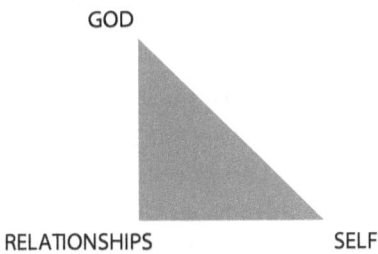

Let me explain the triangle: What is primary and most important is your relationship with yourself and God.

And all other relationships, are a 'means' to express ourselves through them and ultimately reach our goal in life. Not only relationships with family but relationships with all of life is a 'means'. This is when we use relationships for their right reasons. As a mean to connect 'God'. The love of God is so powerful that once you have tasted it, nothing is more fascinating to you.
Enjoy.

From: Antoine Paris
Date: Jul 2, 2016 10:00
Subject: Another email is coming
To: Abeera Shaikh

Hello,
There is an email for you in my drafts. Was about to send it yesterday, but, still, need to complete it. Thanks for sharing your writings.
Let me finish my email and send it to you.
Antoine

From: Antoine Paris

THE GIRL WHO LOVED HERSELF

Date: Jul 2, 2016 10:56
Subject: Second email in a row
To: Abeera Shaikh

How are you? 2 emails in a day. It is close to my world record!

I am tired, though I enjoy Ramadan, and these are the last 10 days. We are so blessed.

Yesterday we had an Iftar (breaking fast in the evening) with my friends and we went to the central mosque for prayers. The meditation was lovely.

I wanted to know when and where we can meet. A long weekend is ideal. I had in mind Istanbul but with the last bombing; I am not sure. It think it is a good idea to go to a place that has more security.

What do you think? We can go to Morocco. Marrakech is nice, but it will be hot – maybe not as much as Dubai. Another idea? Most destinations are hot, but me, I need to go somewhere hot. London has been grey and cold recently.

Timing wise, I have to say the sooner the better. I am keen to go somewhere and relax. So, July looks good for me. August as well. Let us put a date on the calendar! What do you suggest?

I made dua's (invocation) for you last night.

I am not sure about the implications for my job after BREXIT. There will be consequences, but they are hard to predict. But it can mean they might transfer me to Zurich. We are not there yet. I am pragmatic about my job and Zurich is a wonderful place too: mountains, lakes, nature and unpolluted air.

I would like, though, to be more in the flow of things. I accept what is proposed to me but there are a few things where I need to let go more freely, and with increased confidence, it will lead me to the right place where God wants me to be.

Have a wonderful last days of Ramadan and let's finalize a place to travel. Again, as of now, any weekend looks good. I want to plan my summer now that Ramadan is on its last days.

And as regards to your understanding on relationships and Spirituality, I have no doubts. It's amazing you can write this. I have understood this after a lot of introspection. I learned my lessons the hard way. Do you mind me asking how you realized all this?
Take care.
Antoine

From: Abeera Shaikh

Date: Jul 4, 2016 15:26
Subject: Re: Second email in a row
To: Antoine Paris

Hello,

World records, interesting to know.

Yes, Morocco seems fine. Can I suggest Konya? Can we go there? Despite what happened in Turkey, I am drawn to that place.

For BREXIT, you know better, I would say. I should focus more on the news. I can pray that God does well for you. We should rely on Him and trust Him. The mind has a limited perception and the way we calculate things may or may not give us the outcome we perceive, but if we trust, even the tragedies can turn into blessings, and every experience you encounter can only help you evolve and move forward in life. I have learned that.

All right, I will get back to you on the dates, as my HR lady called me to get my visa renewed. Let's see how long that takes. So maybe by the end of July or the first week of August, we can schedule. Would you want to go from Wednesday to Saturday or from Friday to Monday?

So, Ramadan is almost over, and I loved every bit.

I got so exhausted today; I took a day off from work. I can do the remaining things in the apartment today.

I learned these lessons the hard way too. When my personal relationships fell apart. The relationships who I felt were a world for me. The relationships I never thought I could live without. The relationships I was proud of. The relationships I had loved more than myself and more than anyone in this world. These relationships humiliated me, offended me and abused me. But I didn't give up. I stood up for myself, for my respect and for my rights. And the least I expected, they abandoned me.

For many months I felt I would die, every day was a challenge. I used to cry so much that every morning my eyes swelled and I had to hide them at work.

But I turned to God, and when you turn to God, He never leaves you alone.

And then I could not know when and how but everything changed in my sorrowful life.

Life became beautiful, bright, full of colors, and I found that peace my soul had been longing for.

And I realized, everything is temporary. And only by connecting to God one can find true peace.

Ok, bye for now. Keep writing letters.

Have a blessed EID!
Abeera
From: Abeera Shaikh
Date: Jul 6, 2016 19:34
Subject: EID greetings
To: Antoine Paris

Hello,
    Hope you are enjoying EID.
    I went to my cousin's place (Eman and her family) and had celebrations last night.
    EID is a great time after the long month of fasting. So, I celebrated and applied henna on my hands. My mom and my sister sent clothes. I wore one of those outfits and enjoyed.
Abeera

From: Antoine Paris
Date: Jul 6, 2016 at 19:54
Subject: Re: EID greetings
To: Abeera Shaikh

Hello,
    Thanks for your wishes. A very happy EID to you and your family as well.
    I will write back to you this weekend.
    Regarding the long weekend, it is now a moving target on my side. My boss has been changing his holidays a few times. He is out till August 12. The boss is the boss. Maybe we could target the weekend after August 13th or the 20th? Would it be a possibility on your end?
    I am on my way to an EID celebration. We are celebrating EID in a communal garden near Regent's Park. And today is a beautiful sunny day in London.
    May God accept your prayers and acts of worship during this Ramadan.
Antoine

From: Antoine Paris
Date: Jul 6, 2016 1:00
Subject: Re: EID greetings
To: Abeera Shaikh
    Sorry, our emails must have crossed.

Back from EID gathering. Tired but happy.
Antoine
From: Abeera Shaikh
Date: Jul 9, 2016 8:43
Subject: EID celebrations
To: Antoine Paris

Hello

Good morning, so the EID vacations are over. Today is my usual alternate Saturday day off.

I went to Abu Dhabi with a friend yesterday. It's almost 2 hours' drive. I don't know if you have been to Abu Dhabi, but it is worth a visit to see the majestic mosque it was a very impressive visit, as the entrance is free to non-Muslims, and even during prayers the tourist part of the mosque remained open to all visitors! I meditated in the mosque and said my prayers.

So how is your weekend going, and how is your family and where are they? I suppose France.

Take care.
Abeera

From: Antoine Paris
Date: Jul 9, 2016 10:47
Subject: Re: EID celebrations
To: Abeera Shaikh

Bonjour!

Yes, EID is over. Yesterday it was routine, eating lunch in the canteen and drinking coffee.

I am now sitting in a local coffee shop 2 minutes from where I live. The owner is an Algerian, my friend. He works very hard, opens every day at 6am-6.30am and closes the shop at 10 pm.... 7 days a week! Impressive.

I felt sad with Ramadan ending. People say the end of Ramadan is like a friend leaving.

I had a few ego moments this week. Gush, how quick can our mind takes over?

My family is in France. My parents live in Metz though today they are in the south of France. They have a flat next to the seaside. I wanted to join them but the dates didn't work because of my Zurich trip. I need to visit them for a weekend later this summer.

Both my brother and my parents sent me an email wishing me a happy EID. It brightened my heart.

Going now to buy a butter croissant to enjoy further my beginning of the weekend. Yes, I am French.

I have never been to Abu Dhabi.

I am thinking about the Day of Judgment. Sometimes I feel close to God, sometimes I feel far from Him. I guess we are like the tides on the shores trying to make our way as high as possible on the firm ground.

Wish you a great weekend and your emails are always very interesting, and I love and enjoy writing to you.

And sorry I hope you don't mind me asking who these, "relationships" were?
Antoine

From: Abeera Shaikh
Date: Jul 10, 2016 17:03
Subject: Re: Re: EID celebrations
To: Antoine Paris

Hello,

Happy reading!

Wow, French, I should learn French from you. That would be so interesting.

EID is over, yes.

Before I had the understanding that God approves of a certain way and thus I was afraid of God. But now I believe in a loving God. Love is something we as Muslims often forget. When you love someone so much, you don't want to upset them, rather; you want to please them. This is when fear is transformed into love. Here it has a different level of fear. Life is about love, internally and externally for self. And when you do things out of love, it differs from doing things out of fear. When your actions are love based, you put your heart and soul in that, rather than when they are fear-based, where your actions can be defensive, protective, etc.

And yes, my perceptions changed after my relationships went downhill. The relationships I placed on a high pedestal. Unfortunately, they were none other than my father and my brother. Sometimes relationships die even when people are alive. But I agree it was completely my fault to have trusted and loved them above everything, and the worst above myself and God. It is only after I learned the lessons I realized. When you love these relationships so much you have no place in your heart to love God.

Hope you enjoyed reading!
Abeera

-From: Antoine Paris
Date: Jul 13, 2016 3:20
Subject: Weekday news
To: Abeera Shaikh

Hello!

An email even in between weekends. What is going on with me?

This week I should be less under water at work. I should be able to finish around 7pm or maximum 8. One of my friends called me a workaholic, though.

So, yes, I will spend a few days with my parents in Metz. I will visit them on the 30th of July. They have a beautiful house with a nice garden and a view on the hill. It is full of greenery during the summer. My visit to them is usually very relaxing.

And for the trip thing. I got approval from my boss for the 19 to 22 August. True sunshine and enjoying being away from computer and Blackberry. I look forward to seeing you.

I visited Konya in 2015. We can still go there, as you seem to be drawn to the place, which is understandable. There are Rumi and other great saints, but as a classical touristic place, it is limited. We should be able to manage. We can go around the city. The sea is not far, nor Cappadocia.

So, are the days fine with you? I would like to book my flights as soon as possible (by the end of the week latest) to avoid paying heavy prices by booking at the eleventh hour.

The first few days after Ramadan were challenging at work both physically and mentally. I had to take coffee before going to work. Couldn't go straight to work without coffee.

But I have been feeling at peace, also much clearer in my mind and in my heart. The meditation today was strong.

It is true, God has love for us. It is something we overlook too often as Muslims. We focus too much on the warning side of the revelations, which are important too but, yes, God loves us, and we should love God. Remember Him and be grateful to Him. I agree.

I understand about your loss. I feel it was the price for you to, "pay" and to make room to love God and for God's love to take dominance. It is as if you had to destroy some of these loves, or better to say you had to go through a transformational phase. Where God's love dominates. I am sure it must have been challenging but God will reward you. And the lessons you have learned are the truth about life. You are lucky you have learned these lessons so early in life. I am happy for you. I know many people who continuously struggle in relationships but never find salvation.

I think about my consciousness 10 years ago and what it is now. I can hardly believe who I was 10 years ago.

I have got a busy schedule tomorrow at work then the weekend is on the horizon.

Do you stay up late at night? This early morning when I did my meditation at 3:30am, cross- legged on my sofa, in my living room, I felt like I belonged to another planet. I feel I need to better understand my intuitions. And so, when these moments happen, I like to take time to savor them and internalize them. Phases of reflection are important steps in life.

Feels like I have a lot more to say but don't find it easy to put these emotions or intuitions in words right now.

Oh, and I have a question. Do you believe in spiritual love? That someone somewhere is made for you?

Wish you blessed days and nights.
Antoine

From: Abeera Shaikh
Date: Jul 16, 2016 9:00
Subject: Re: Weekday news
To: Antoine Paris

Hello,

Thanks for your email. It is always a pleasure to hear from you. Now enjoy reading!

Thinking what to wear on my Birthday, i.e. tomorrow, 17 July. (A very happy birthday to me, the most amazing woman on this earth, LOL.)

We often get so busy in our mundane lives we forgot to celebrate. I am planning a day off to pamper myself: massage, Jacuzzi, steam bath and facial, a day for me to celebrate turning 32.

I called the HR to start the process for my visa renewal. I need to have a minimum of 6 months validity for my Dubai visa before I can apply for a visa to travel. Let's see how long that would take, and we can go ahead with the bookings.

Through my experiences I have come to understand love comes from God. It is only God who puts love in the hearts of His people. And it is only God who can take that love back. It is not in our controls.

Only God knows what lies in our hearts.

For the spiritual love, many people believe it is formed for the ultimate reunion with God. Spiritual love is where the basis of the relationship is your spiritual goals for you and your partner. Some of my friends in meditation have unusual love stories. But very few people are lucky to form a relationship for God. Even though our marriage vows say we accept it in the name of God.

I want to go to Konya to feel the energy of that place.

I offer my condolences to the families of what happened in France recently.

Enjoy your weekend, take care.

PS: Can I make a request, please? (Hope you don't mind, my sincere apologies if you do.) Can you change the timings of your emails, please? Whenever you send me emails between 1 am-4am, Dubai time I wake up from my sleep, even though my phone is on vibration. That's weird, as emails rarely disturb me. Though, I wait to hear from you.

PS2: Enjoy your family visit!

PS3: Yeah, I am a night owl, ever since my childhood. Love the silence of the night much before I started meditation.

PS4: Just heard something not well in Turkey. Don't think there are many safe places to visit. I should rather apply for UK visa (though it can be very difficult on my Pakistani passport), or you can come to Dubai anytime.

Chapter 10

God's Planning

THE GIRL WHO LOVED HERSELF

From: Antoine Paris
Date: Jul 17, 2016 11:14
Subject: Joyeux Anniversaire (Happy birthday)
To: Abeera Shaikh

Hello,

Happy Birthday to you. I wish you a blessed day and a blessed upcoming year.

Yes, 32 is a beautiful age and you are going into your 33rd year... a symbolic age... the age of Prophet Jesus in the Bible and Isa (May Peace Be Upon Him) in the Quran when God took him from Earth back to Heaven. And I have read that for those who have lived over 33 years, to honor Prophet Jesus in the Bible and Isa (May Peace Be Upon Him) in the Quran, our appearance on the day of the resurrection will be the one we had at that age.

I wanted to share a word with you. These are words from Rumi, and, when reading your last email, I understand why you are drawn to the place, i.e., Konya. Maybe I am reading too much into it, but I couldn't help draw parallels yesterday. Rumi said to his people but also to the whole of humanity that:

Your task is not to seek for love, but merely to seek and find all the barriers within yourself that you have built against it.

It feels like you are in full resonance, so to speak, with his saying, and that you have experienced that journey where now you have unravelled the barriers, and you are filled with love, hope and gratitude. Love for God but also love for yourself (in a pure and non-egoistic way). It is only the beginning of your journey, but you are immensely blessed to embark on a genuine spiritual path leading to truth, so early in life.

Wish you again a wonderful day. Enjoy it – I am sure you will.
Antoine
PS: Will reply to you later in the week about yesterday's email.
PS2: Dubai it is. Never been there and I am not afraid of the heat! I am booking the flight. Will send you the details soon. Do you know which hotel(s) is best suited, i.e. near your place, etc.?

From: Abeera Shaikh
Date: Jul 17, 2016 16:00
Subject: Re: Joyeux Anniversaire
To: Antoine Paris

Hello,

Thanks, a very quick reply!

I came to Pakistan this morning around 5 am, just booked my tickets and came right away, just like me, full of surprises and following my heart.

Yes, you can go ahead with your bookings whenever it is convenient for you. There are three airports and all of them are close to my apartment. I don't mind picking you up.

For a hotel, any hotel in Dubai Marina. This should be most convenient, otherwise any other hotel you prefer to stay at shouldn't be an issue, as I can be your guide.

Let me know if you want to know anything else.

Ok, I need to get ready for the dinner, family get together and the birthday celebration.

I should be back to Dubai on Saturday. You can email me anytime while I am here.

Bye
Abeera

From: Abeera Shaikh
Date: Jul 19, 2016 at 18:08
Subject: Birthday and the family
To: Antoine Paris

Hello,

Last year when I came to Pakistan my inward journey to God had already begun, but it's challenging when you have an injured soul and resentment built for years.

I learned, compassion for others help you understand them.

My aunt advised me, "Have patience, God loves those who have patience and God has great rewards for those who have patience."

I learned patience also.

Some experiences teach you forgiveness, patience and love for God.

And now, I have many male friends, who express their love in different ways. I have my boundaries, but they are amazing people who take care of me and are very concerned about me.

It's so romantic to see people going gaga crazy over me (LOL).

Ok, bye for now.

Abeera

THE GIRL WHO LOVED HERSELF

From: Antoine Paris
Date: Jul 21, 2016 19:58
Subject: London - Zurich - London
To: Abeera Shaikh

Hello,

    I am not surprised that you have a "cour de pretendants" (circling around you). Not in order of priority or in order of preference, you are smart, lively, educated, engaging, sparkly, independent, etc. So, for sure, especially if we translate those qualities in a "Muslim" context... you got the heads of many males spinning and spinning. I really laughed when you wrote "gaga." Cute. Even in a Western context, heads would spin for you.

    The obvious transition there is the difference between Eastern and Western values regarding the relationship between men and women and what are the expectations, boundaries, attitudes and codes.

    And here I was last summer, after I reverted, having to comprehend being alone or single, feeling I will have to climb Mount Everest to find a spouse for myself. But deep inside I had faith that God will bring me to the right person for me and I need not worry. It's a matter of faith. I think the biggest challenge in today's world is not only for people who don't believe in God but also for people who believe in God. To believe that there is a God and have faith in God are two different things. We often confuse them. Believing in God just means you believe in a God who exists whether that is for Muslims or other religions. But having faith in God is the real thing. I am not saying one should sit hand on hand and allow miracles to happen. Though miracles can happen if we have faith.

    I too believe spirituality should be the center and the reason for relationships. Spirituality is lacking, and so societies are where they are in terms of relationships and also in other aspects, but we need to redefine/transform to understand the real meanings of relationships, not the way we had comprehended them.

    And gratitude is very important. When you have gratitude for all that God has given you, you don't have to worry about anything.

    I am impressed by your current state. You put God at the center of everything.

    And last time when I told you I wanted to share more with you but didn't really know what to say or where to start, it was because I felt we had exhausted our discussions. It is ridiculous to say because there are so many dimensions to what we have discussed that it is as if we are building a deep pond to swim in. But that's how I felt and I didn't know where to start, what to start with. And then

God's Planning

your email of last weekend came in. And bang! It opened the gates of inspiration again. I remember writing a long response to you over the weekend - in my head - but then got dragged into housekeeping matters and got very busy on Sunday and Monday.

I had to wake up at 3am to get the 6am flight to Zurich on Tuesday. I was so tired that I put four alarms on my smartphone and another one on my Blackberry, too afraid I would sleep in and miss my flight. I was walking like a zombie when I woke up on that morning.

I spent three days in Zurich. It was, overall, good.

Anyway, I am in the plane and soon to land at Heathrow, writing to you and feeling good about it.

So next weekend (end of the month) I am in Metz. I will have a relaxing time with my parents and my grandmother.

So, all booked.

And for Dubai, all booked too. I land on Thursday 18 of August at 21:25pm.

I depart on Monday 22 late in the evening.

I stay in Dubai Marina - sounds like I got a good deal and you told me it would be most convenient. So here it is. Dubai was the last place I was expecting to spend a long weekend this summer. But here it is. Never say never.

I look at the clouds over London; it reminds me I had no time to take photos in Zurich. Twice I had to go for dinner with my boss and I got very late..

I have landed and now I am polishing my email sitting in a cab. The driver is friendly. I am enjoying talking to him.

Tonight, it is back to meditation practice. I have been too busy in Zurich. When you go back to your hotel room at midnight after a hard day of work, it is hard to meditate.

I hope you continue to have a blissful stay in Pakistan with your family.

Take care
Antoine

From: Abeera Shaikh
Date: Jul 23, 2016 21:53
Subject: Dubai is Dubai
To: Antoine Paris

Hello,

I wanted to spend more time with my brother's daughter – it never seems enough. The first time the baby stayed with us overnight and she is a sweetheart.

THE GIRL WHO LOVED HERSELF

I enjoyed seeing my family.

I am missing my apartment, made with so much love.

Damn, this airport is so crowded and there are so many flights to Dubai. Dubai is the place where I have seen the best of people. You develop an association with the place where you learn a lot. I learned to live alone, to be independent, to open my eyes wide and then as wide as I could. I discovered my passion – my passion for writing – made peace with solitude, enjoying my single life to its fullest and learned to trust God above all. The Arabs have changed a desert into an amazing city that provides employment to so many people across the globe, a city full of security with a good life standard, and technology. I am impressed.

I am in the plane, still writing and loving it.

And when I look at myself 10 years ago, I laugh at myself. I was a different person.

A few hours for dinners would still be less than enough time to discuss my writings (LOL). Our first encounter was for three hours yet seemed so short (LOL). The plane is landing. I am in Dubai. The temperature is 39 degrees centigrade. Once upon a time, I used to buy drinks from duty free (LOL).

I sense a different energy within me, free and relaxed.

I smiled when I read your comment. God is the center of everything. Everything.

You are right. I have learned the relationship of a man with God is that of faith, trust and surrender. Because of our weak faiths. We are insecure. And because of our insecurities we don't believe God has abundance resources. Thus, we lie, cheat, hurt, snatch, etc.

I recently wrote these questions one can ask themselves about their faith. I learned them through my personal experiences.

Do you have faith that no matter what may happen God will take care of you, protect you, provide you and do everything for you?

Do you have faith you need no one except God?

Do you have faith that every time you ask, God answers?

Have you ever tried to build that relationship of faith with God?

Have you ever spent a while turning to God and allowed the answers to come to you?

Enjoy

From: Antoine Paris

Date: Jul 26, 2016 20:31
Subject: Re: Dubai is Dubai
To: Abeera Shaikh

Hello,

I am again heart warmed that you had a lovely time with your family. I am looking forward to my turn this weekend. It will be relaxing. If the weather is fine, breakfasts/lunches will be in the garden. The day is ahead, full of its promises and wonders.

I fasted for the first time after Ramadan yesterday, and today I am enjoying my morning coffee.

Maybe I can share with you more thoughts on the notion of why there is the flow of our conversation, its quality, why it feels special and unique. I am a writer too. I forgot that when I was a young boy, I also wanted to write a book. At Christmas, I even got a gift which was a toolkit for wannabee writers. I even wrote a couple of pages.

Anyway, this is another beautiful illustration of the love of God which is flowing all over us.

I guess the flow led me to sharing that to you this morning.

I really liked the questions you wrote about faith.

Enjoy your day.

Antoine

PS: When I was about to email you, my batteries ran out. I thought it was interesting. Does it mean something?

PS2: I panicked. I am used to reading the Qur'an in the tube and sometimes write emails. So, a smartphone is essential for my commute.

PS3: I told myself how dependant we are on those things. 45 minutes without my phone is not the end of the world.

PS4: It allowed me to think, ponder on many things, and it led to very interesting realizations and thoughts, so there was a reason for my batteries to run out.

From: Abeera Shaikh
Date: Jul 27, 2016 23:32
Subject: Re: Dubai is Dubai
To: Antoine Paris

Hello,

Anyways, what do you mean, "Maybe share with you more thoughts on the notion of why there is flow of our conversation, its quality, why it feels special and unique?" And I will ignore it.

I laughed while reading your email. 45 minutes is not the end of the world without your phone. It's true, we are so attached to our phones. But technology is beautiful if you have used your time enriching your heart and soul, for learning or for self-development.

Maybe we can write a book together someday if so God pleases. I intuitively felt you were a writer too.

And yes, during Ramadan when you said, "Too many intuitions and emotions," I had an idea, and you also mentioned strong meditation. I don't understand whether to call it intuitions or telepathy, but it is not new for me. Ever since I was young, I would intuitively feel a lot of things about many people, and it's strange and unique at the same time.

Had a long day at work and a training too, came home, did my meditation and prayers. Can't resist writing to you, even though I am exhausted.

I feel that we have made everything a concept. Religion. God. Love. Relationships. Self. Whereby everything is an experience for self. God is not a concept. Religion is not a concept. Love is not a concept nor is self a concept. When we make things into a concept, we follow them mechanically. We don't understand. We don't evolve. We don't grow. We follow that which others have been following without questioning and without gaining the required knowledge. Life is an experience of self.

All that one needs to do is listen to one's heart where God's desire for you is. Without judging yourself and defending yourself to anyone. One can only do this when they love themselves unconditionally and completely. Have you ever expressed love for yourself?

Take care
Abeera

From: Antoine Paris
Date: Jul 30, 2016 21:05
Subject: Quelques Nouvelles (Some News)
To: Abeera Shaikh

Hello,

I am in France with my parents and my grandmother (90 years old). Just prayed and I am going for a short run to stretch and leave the stress of the week behind. Friday was a nice day but very challenging at work.

Before I used to wonder if, "God needs us, and God has created us to worship Him. Which had scared me a lot." But now I realize that all the worship we do is for us. There are three tools to connect to God:
1. Prayer: Prayer is the highest form of worship. By praying you are connecting yourself to the real source 'God'.
2. Meditation: Meditation helps you silence your mind and align with your truth by freeing yourself through the constructs of your mind and beliefs that no longer work for you.
3. Remembrance (Zikr): To awaken your heart by remembering God.

And yes, when I mentioned "unique," it was just referring to my intuitions. We have already meditated together, we follow the same meditation group and that creates a bond. 100%. That is what I meant. That is why it has flown so much. Intense at some points. Yes. But when two hearts open, the field of communication and sharing is vast. Should we dare to say limitless?

You, me, us, the blessings of Ramadan, the limitations can become blurry, as all dilutes in God ultimately.

Anyway, two things before I go.

First, I can't wait to get to you and see Dubai. Let us discuss the program next week. I am simple and laid back. I am here for the company and enjoy the spirit of the place. I am not a tick the box tourist. Quite the opposite. But still, let us see what could be most interesting to do.

I had in mind we could treat ourselves in a nice restaurant one evening. I can bring my suit and we could celebrate in a fine dining experience. What do you think?

No, I had three things to tell you.

The last, and I am serious about it, I felt last week and last weekend when we had all these exchanges and intimate letters; I needed to hug you. There was a need to share at the physical level the energy created at the spiritual level. Voilà. (Satisfied)
Hugs ***
Antoine

From: Abeera Shaikh
Date: Jul 31, 2016 23:52
Subject: Re: Quelques Nouvelles
To: Antoine Paris
Hello,

I barely know what to write but as usual it will be a long letter.

It is such a lovely feeling writing to you again and the state I am in, every word seems a low-rated word: ecstasy, overwhelmed, tuned in, tapped in, turned on, on Cloud 9, seeing the blessings and God everywhere.

So yes, let me share the fun part now. I got worried when I could feel your "hugs" without you mentioning and a lot more. Well, maybe that's the heart-to-heart thing. God knows, damn, I got worried; I don't intend to give any attention to this physical energy. But, yes, now I can say I won't mind being in your arms all day long (LOL, I am there already).

And this state of your presence with me was so obvious, my friends could sense it. I was wondering if these emails impacted me. I am often so lost in them; I smile for no reason, and my colleagues just can't understand what's going on, but they know something is happening. My friends are worried about me as I am so out of touch with everybody.

Enjoy your stay.

Regards to your family.

Thank you.

Abeera.

From: Antoine Paris
Date: Aug 3, 2016 22:09
Subject: Goodbye France
To: Abeera Shaikh

Hello.

I didn't know what to say, but, like you, inspiration and words have flowed again.

First things first. I didn't answer earlier your so tender email because I was focused on my work. And my mind was busy with these deadlines. In retrospect, it was silly of me, but I got stuck. I had to deal with those deadlocks to free myself up and be ready to write you back. In the grand scheme of things, they represent little, but they got me stressed. The atmosphere at work is getting heavier, and that is unpleasant. I want everything to be perfect. One of my boss's really challenges me at work and sometimes it becomes very difficult.

Anyway, this morning I had two back-to-back "important" presentations at the bank, and I couldn't work on those in France because my laptop didn't connect. Another IT glitch. I ended up feeling stressed and had to come to work at 6 am yesterday morning. Though these two presentations went well.

But let's come back to us.

I need to tell you one thing now. Now you have mentioned spending a day in my arms, well, my desire to visit anything in Dubai has vanished. Please motivate me.

Oh! I shared your regards to my family.

And that leads me to an interesting moment of my weekend. For the first time, I have discussed "the future" with my mum and my grandmother, late in the afternoon on Saturday. I was about to go for a run near the river which flows close to our house.

I explained my conditions, my possibilities, my boundaries. We spoke for over 30 minutes on the subject. It relieved my mum. I had to give details about the boundaries which prevail for observing Muslims. Did I tell you that my family is still Christian?

So yes, a lot of discussions about geopolitics, local politics and religion. Overall, it went well.

What was harder is when we had to re-discuss the moment where I told my mum why I reverted, the background, the different steps of the spiritual journey. I suspect that I will have to address it again. I pray that my mum has a better sense of everything now. It is all positive, but her perception can be different. I thank God because the link of kinship has not broken despite me being a Muslim. But now, they know about Friday prayers, the different prayers (more or less) and they buy halal meat for me. That is great.

And then this moment: my mother and I walked along the ancient walls of the city. My mum spoke for a few minutes about some of her friends, anecdotes of past holidays. All that looked very distant for me and not very interesting… But I reminded myself how important the relationship is with my parents, how important it is to nurture and respect my parents. I changed my state of mind. I told myself that it was a special moment. My mum and I were strolling gently under the sun and having many discussions. They were moments to cherish. I felt happy and blessed.

And I am impressed with your letter again. I am fasting today. In the tube, on my way home. I am tired, words don't come easy. I am slow in my mind but happy in my heart. I lack energy.
Antoine

From: Abeera Shaikh
Date: Aug 5, 2016 14:12
Subject: Re: Goodbye France

THE GIRL WHO LOVED HERSELF

To: Antoine Paris

Hello,

Hmm, a lot to share in the professional area too, but all I have realized is: if one focuses on their spiritual growth, every area benefits and becomes easier to handle.

Often the lessons we most need to learn, come to us from people who challenge us. I have learned a lot on the professional side. My previous boss was very difficult. I learned that to develop patience; we need to be in situations where patience is required.

To practice compassion, we need to experience situations where compassion is required.

To learn where our growing edges are, we need to be pushed to the edge. When you get annoyed with someone, take time to see what the situation is calling of you.

While these times and people may not feel particularly pleasant, they come to you for your spiritual development.

Rather than getting upset, angry or feeling uncomfortable: Stop. Breathe. Relax. Pray. Reflect.

Ask yourself these questions:
1. What is this person here to teach me in this moment?
2. What are you required to practice with this person?
3. How can you create peace in this situation?

You are always provided opportunities to practise love, patience, gratitude, acceptance, forgiveness, and peace. That's the real work to do in every situation of life.

Abeera shares her personal story with him about her journey to experience God's presence through the betrayal of her loved ones.
See you soon.
Abeera

From: Antoine Paris
Date: Aug 8, 2016 19:16
Subject: Before I meditate
To: Abeera Shaikh

Hello,

Before I meditate, I can't help but reach out to you with a few words, saying,

I think of you, us, tonight, tomorrow and next week.
   Have a sweet and blessed night.
Bye.
Antoine

From: Antoine Paris
Date: Aug 15, 2016 21:12
Subject: Airport
To: Abeera Shaikh

Hello,
   I fly to you via Oman. I land in Terminal 1 at 21:25 this Thursday... Flight WY611.
Sweet night to you.
Antoine

From: Antoine Paris
Date: Aug 18, 2016 6:33
Subject: Dragons
To: Abeera Shaikh

Bonjour! (Hello)
   Here I am. Checked-in. Gone through security and now enjoying a light breakfast at Apostrophe. I have to say, Heathrow looks amazing after they have redone it. I enjoy going to Heathrow. Part of the trip experience. It is early now, and it is silent. I am enjoying it.
   Yesterday was super busy at work. I wanted to clear as much as possible to get my head cleared from work issues. Guess what? The boss who I mentioned earlier kept me very busy. I tried to give him a five-star service. And you know what? At the end I got a "Great, thanks" from him. And my boss replied: "Top!!" Isn't this interesting? Thank you for your email. Actually, I looked at his behavior positively and it really helped.
   With packing and rushing home, there has been little time to think. But I was thinking about how princes in the past used to conquer their princesses. It was a tough journey: going through dark forests, with witches trying to seduce them on their way, and the dragons. Slaying a dragon was a necessity on the path to the loved one. Or maybe multiple dragons if the princess was really amazingly beautiful.

THE GIRL WHO LOVED HERSELF

And what did I do today? Well, I booked a ticket online, booked a cab in the morning, and drove smoothly to the airport and not to mention checking in takes time and tests your patience, with people in front of you with heavy pieces of luggage. I wonder what they put in it.

Ok, it is a long flight but there is entertainment and I am enjoying writing to you.

Where is my dragon to slay? I need one or two.

Ok. I stop there, though I couldn't help but draw a parallel between the prince's adventures and ours on the spiritual path. If you take everything at the symbolic level, well, our path is not so dissimilar to the one of a prince and a princess.

We have our dark places, witches, distractions, weak spots, etc. And ego is our dragon. We need a constant fight with the ego (NAFS as we Muslims call it). The real foundation of a relationship should be the spiritual aspects, its challenges and its rewards. So before I meet you I want to share many things with you. Thank you for sharing your story.

Pondering on our letters, I have to say I could not help but compare practices with fibre optics. We have reached a level of communication and sharing which might have taken months (or even years?) to reach for a normal relationship. What do you think? I have to say this realization is astonishing. It means that hearts can connect instantly; sharing of feelings, emotions and words start on different levels. It is as if the download starts and does not stop when hearts are clicking. Anyway, another proof that in the realm of the spiritual, the notion of time and space are challenged by what we have on earth. Also, it means that at the spiritual level, exchange happens more rapidly than in the realm of the mind. That is why suddenly we talked and discussed matters which we would have never thought we were capable of.

And for your story. I want to push the metamorphosis further – and I am using comparison at the strictly pure symbolic level – to be crystal clear, I would say your father's love was the figure of command/order/reassurance/etc. Could we say it has been "replaced or repositioned" with God's love? And for your brother, well, you mentioned confidence/sharing of words/intimacy. I would say this transformation has – maybe – made room for you to welcome and embrace with your heart a true lover. That is maybe why things did not unfold as expected beforehand. That is how I felt at the end. I hope you see no rudeness or clumsiness in this interpretation of mine. I could not help but think about that at the end of the reading!

And yes the EGO (NAFS) loves quarrel, loves aggressiveness, loves barking and hurting. There are even people called vampires, not because they are born somewhere hidden in Romania but because they feed on others' pain and suffering. They are energy vampires. It reflects their own inner states, which are not satisfactory, but the way they deal with it is to go out there, so to speak, and to attract and to feed on the positivity of others by lashing out negatively. By doing so, they consciously or unconsciously trap the positive energy of their surroundings and feel satisfied – at least for a short period only – and that is why they have to keep on repeating their behavior. Honestly, I was like that when I was younger. It is only now I recognize it. The power of the meditation and prayers have its transformational effects on us. It never stops to fascinate me.

Now I am so much more ready to share my love and express it. Before I was hiding it, too afraid to show it because it could expose me and make me feel weak. Sharing love is truly a magnificent act.

And yes, to get peace of the soul is very difficult but once reached it is the true self. It is grounded, beautiful, and peaceful. And to reach this stage we have to fight with our Nafs. Your story is beautiful. Finally, your soul got the peace it was longing for, and that peace can only come by turning to God. So it means we are intrinsically good as long as our hearts and souls are peaceful. This is the state where we connect to our inner being and/or God. I am very happy for you. Love yourself is an incomplete story unless you connect to the source and that source is no other than 'God'.

Bon, switching now to a more "terre à terre" (down to earth) matter.

So here I am, coming to you, not a white knight in a shining armour in the literal sense but a heart pure enough.
See you soon.
Antoine

So, it's Thursday. Tonight, he is coming. With mixed emotions, Abeera was wondering how it will go. She thought: *I met him on a retreat, but people are different on retreats, I suppose. I have this little clumsy girl inside me. In emails it seems I am grounded and a mature woman. Besides, he is the first European I have ever connected with. The emails had an immense flow. But I wonder how we will be in person? Or is this just because I am a writer?*

From: Antoine Paris
Date: Aug 18, 2016 12:08
Subject: Rebooking
To: Abeera Shaikh

I missed my connecting flight. Rebooking will be done by a team in Muscat. So basically, I don't know when I can arrive in Dubai until I land in Muscat.

I checked online and there are one or two flights leaving from Muscat to Dubai at 11:30 pm.

So earliest I can arrive in Dubai is at 00:30 am, or after that, it is 3:00 am or later. Fun!

I guess it is best you don't wait for me as there are too many unknown factors.

I will send you a note when I got re-booked in Muscat, and it feels like we will see each other for breakfast then.

Sweet Kiss.
Antoine

After she received Antoine's email. Abeera walked in her room and thought, he *seems so relaxed, and here I am confused and nervous. It is hard to understand myself. For a minute I am excited, and the next minute I am puzzled.*

Imran called, "Hey, are you happy?"

With astonishment, Abeera replied, "Happy about what?"

"The French guy is coming tonight."

"Oh! You still remember. Happiness in relationships is not meant for me. Life is a series of twists for me. I am so immune to the sadness in my life that when something good happens, I take a while to accept it. I'm worried. I should be delighted, but I'm not. I rather feel I should stay confident, grounded, mature, and not lose myself in him, no matter how good he is."

Imran smiled on the phone and replied, "Don't worry. I am sure everything will go well."

"Ok, thanks, Imran. I'll get back to you later. Please pray for me."

From: Abeera Shaikh
Date: Aug 18, 2016 01:48
Subject: Re: Re-booking
To: Antoine Paris

I will pick you up. Don't worry.

Let me know when you reach the airport here. It shouldn't take you long to come out.

Hope you eat something, not surviving only on your coffee.

Take care.
Abeera

PS: Thank you for your comments on my story. Ego is one of the biggest challenges on the path to God. This experience was one of the best experiences of my life. Perhaps challenging and painful but that does not matter when you can look back and smile. Often I smile and thank God. I am blessed.

Abeera was again nervously walking in her room, *if Antoine is expecting a girl who is interested in a needy and romantic love, or a relationship where I would go head over heels for him. Perhaps that won't happen. I am not looking for a partner, for a romantic love story. But, yes, I am looking for God's will, God's sign, and praying for His will to be revealed to me. Having said this, deep inside, I trust no one. I want God, in whom I put my trust.*

From: Antoine Paris
Date: Aug 18, 2016 at 2:00
Subject: Re: Re-booking
To: Abeera Shaikh

Ok. It says now 3:15 or 3:30 am. I will send you a note when I land in Dubai. But please, if you feel sleepy and tired, don't risk driving. Security first; I mean it. See you very soon.
Antoine

Abeera takes shower and dresses up in her beautiful stripped white and blue trousers, sleeveless blue shirt and a white jacket, and went to the airport to pick him up.

Abeera keeps reminding herself, *I have to be aware all along with him.*

She reached the airport early in the morning at 4:00 am. She waited nearly forty minutes at Costa for Antoine to come out. It was difficult to understand her emotions. Her heart was pounding, and her breathing was shallow.

From: Antoine Paris
Date: Aug 19, 2016 4:35
Subject: Come
To: Abeera Shaikh

I am outside in 10 minutes. Come.
Antoine

Chapter 11

The Spiritual Love

Antoine came out of the airport.

They gazed intently into each other's eyes. Abeera blushed.

Awfully nervous, Abeera asked while strolling her hair, "Hey! What took you so long?"

"Sorry to have kept you waiting, but there was a long queue at immigration." He smiled and replied.

They waked to the parking. Abeera felt nervous all the way. Driving someone was not new for her, but this relationship was a unique relationship. Abeera asked him how the flight was.

"It was long, especially because I missed my flight. But I could sleep in the plane. I had a long day at work." He replied with a soft tone.

Even his tone was irresistible. The overloaded sweetness of his French accent.

He looked exhausted because of the long flight but he was very attractive, and, in fact, irresistible.

Abeera drove him to the hotel. She parked her car in the underground parking of her apartment while he checked in.

They did prayers. She prayed in her room and he prayed in the hotel.

After prayers, Abeera went straight to the hotel lobby. They didn't exchange mobile numbers. Abeera wasn't sure if Antoine's number worked on roaming. She didn't ask.

Abeera secretly stared at Antoine several times. She had never seen him so closely. He was tall and gorgeously good looking. She had never dreamed of being with a French guy.

Abeera felt strangely energetic and excited even though all night she could barely sleep.

In the morning Abeera emailed him to confirm.

From: Abeera Shaikh
Date: Aug 19, 2016 8:01
Subject: Good morning
To: Antoine Paris

    Good morning.
    I should see you at 9:00 am? Ok.

From: Antoine Paris
Date: Aug 19, 2016 8:20
Subject: Re: Good morning
To: Abeera Shaikh

Morning!
Yes, we meet at 9:00 am.
Cheers

Abeera picked him up at 9:00 am and headed to a mall nearby for breakfast.

They chatted in the car. Abeera was trying hard not to get carried away with his beautiful looks. He looked calm, composed, and confident.

While she was driving he asked, "How are you feeling?"

"Quite good," she mumbled.

"Did you get some sleep?" he asked while he puts on the CD player.

"Yes. After I dropped you off, I could sleep for two hours. And you? How is the hotel, good?"

"Yeah, yeah, it's good."

Was he private, or was it my crazy feeling that he was hiding his feelings and his thoughts?

He glanced at her and smiled. Gosh! What was he thinking?

Abeera drove as fast as she could to the mall. They reached the mall and went to Starbucks.

They ordered breakfast. Indeed, he was a French guy. He ordered Croissant and Americano. Abeera ordered Chai Latte and a muffin. Antoine paid for the breakfast. Abeera was expecting him to split the bill. Abeera had heard about Westerner's that they do not pay for a woman unless they are committed to her. Anyway, she tried not to think too much about that. Antoine pulled a chair for Abeera to sit. They sat down.

Abeera asked Antoine, "Does anyone in London know you are here?"

"Well, actually, no one. I didn't disclose our relationship to anyone. I don't like when people gossip. I like to stay private."

"Ok. Did you enjoy writing emails?" Abeera asked.

He replied while taking the sip of his coffee, "Enjoyed is a small word. I loved them terribly. Falling in love through letter writing has been going on for hundreds of years, I guess. Online relationships are an improved version of a writing-based relationship. In the new version, the time gap between writing, sending, receiving, and reading has become negligible – I received your reply in the same state that I would send it. This is of great emotional significance."

"I have never written, so many emails to anyone in my life, but I have to say it was a beautiful experience." She replied and picked up the muffin to eat.

They discussed about London, Dubai, their mutual friends from the meditation group and particularly, their emails.

They came back to the hotel after breakfast. He looked tired. In fact, Abeera was tired too. She couldn't sleep the whole night, rolling around the bed, waiting for him to arrive. She didn't want to miss picking him up. That was not all. She was also trying to gather herself together from the last episode of what had happened in her life.

They went to the hotel room after breakfast. Abeera ironed his shirt. She laughed inside and thought *am I already behaving like his wife?* He went for shower and Abeera left his room, trying hard not to get close physically.

Abeera went to her apartment, changed, and then they went to the mosque for Friday prayers. This mosque was a few minutes' drive away. It was not a grand mosque, quite smaller than the one Abeera used to go in Ramadan. But she had also been to this mosque many times after she moved into the new apartment. Even this mosque was close to her heart and soul.

Abeera went into the women's section. There were few ladies in the mosque. Abeera was wearing a lemon-colored sun flower printed, Pakistani style shirt with beautiful beige trousers, feeling as light in her heart as the color of her clothes.

Abeera asked in her prayers, *"God, I hope everything goes well. Please put in my heart what You desire for me. If this is Your desire for me, please put in my heart. Your desire is my desire. My treasure is in my heart where You live."*

They came back from prayers and meditated together in the hotel. The forty-five minutes in meditation went quick, and right afterwards, Abeera went into his bed. What did that mean? For Abeera, she only wanted to sleep. She pulled his hand and asked him to come on the bed. He told her, she should not pull him into this. But she knew she was strong, and she only wanted to hug him tightly and sleep.

But it all happened so fast. She was in his arms and he was holding her tightly against his chest. It was intoxicating. There she was, gazing at him, mesmerized by the strange pull towards him.

She had been fantasizing about the two of them together so deeply, so closely, so madly loving each other. What was in her imagination was now coming true.

She wanted to hide in his arms, even though the room was dark. She looked at him, kissed his face, a gentle soft kiss, while the fingers of his hand softly traced her face, gently probing, a burning gaze for a moment, and eventually, her attention is drawn to his mouth. And for the first time in years, she had no control over herself. He locked her lips in his kiss and she had completely lost herself in him.

Abeera had never liked a lip-to-lip kiss. Abeera had always wondered what pleasure people got out of it, and here she was, lost in his kiss. It was the longest kiss she had ever had. She felt as if no man in the world could ever kiss the way he did, or maybe it was because they were connected through their hearts and souls, maybe this was a sign. She still didn't know if he was the desire of her heart that she had longed for?

After a while, she shook her head. There was tingling in her head. She felt as though she was on some other planet. She asked him, "What have you done?" It was an out-of-body experience, like she had sometimes felt in meditation. She felt embarrassed and immediately left the hotel room.

In the evening, he emailed her and asked for the plan for the evening and also wrote, "Please don't be embarrassed. I am sorry. But I had no control over myself."

Abeera replied to him, "It is fine, I will pick you up in the evening at 6 pm." They went to Burj Khalifa, enjoyed the view of the dancing fountain and had dinner. He held her hand in his hands. The kiss had broken the physical barrier between them. Yet, in the night, Antoine slept in the hotel and she slept in her room.

In the night Abeera dreamed, "Life is (me + you = US)."

The next day they woke up. Abeera wore a black jeans and a red t-shirt, topped with a small necklace and earrings. They met in the hotel lobby and went for breakfast at Starbucks again. The conversations were amazing, punctuated with his lovely kisses. She knew nothing. She kept looking at this man in awe. The communication flew. These moments were precious. She was now feeling comfortable and safe with him.

The communication flew not only in emails but also in person. While driving, she told him, "I have read our emails countless times. They are close to my heart." He smiled, "Me too. Thank you for your lovely long and very long *emails. The pleasure is mine. So when are you writing a book?*"

"I wrote a book a few years back. But for the last few years I have been sorting out my life and relationships. But hopefully, soon, if that is what God wants from me."

"But is it not your own will as well?" he smiled.

"Indeed, it is, but for me nothing exists outside the will of God."

"You are right. I love the way you speak, write and have so much clarity in life. I have the same understanding of God as you. I have to say, I really enjoy all these deep discussions with you. I did not tell you but before reverting to Islam I was lost and confused. My heart broke several times. I had many desires from running after money, women and status in life. But only to realize that we are travellers. This life is nothing but an illusion, and we are nothing but travellers."

"Thank you. Isn't that amazing to know? It is a very important realization. I understand what you mean." Abeera replied.

"Indeed" he said and continued, "Good and bad are just the perceptions of the mind. Everything is a part of the plan of God for the grandest purpose of life. I am very happy with my life. I have realized that the moment you seek yourself in the future and so desperately want to hold on to this moment or a relationship, it becomes a struggle."

"I agree. Every time I was with a man, I wanted a commitment so desperately that I always pushed them away. Life is not meant to be a struggle. Life is meant to be enjoyed. Life is meant to be lived without effort. By enjoying the fun of it. By wanting something so desperately we push it away. That's a lesson I learned after ages of struggle in my life. Our only struggle, if there ever is one, is to align ourselves with what God wants for us. I have left everything to God to decide for me. I'm certain He will do the best for me. All I have to do is relax, enjoy, pray, and breathe." She replied while parking the car.

"Yes, all you have to do is enjoy this moment. Enjoy the process of life as long as you can. Enjoy what you do. Enjoy engaging with people. Savor it. But never seek yourself into it. Whenever you seek yourself in someone. It is not you, it is Ego seeking itself. What is yours will come to you easily! You will not have to chase or struggle." He replied while they headed for breakfast.

The conversation between them was getting deeper and deeper. They talked animatedly, like lost souls reunited after long partying. Abeera loved expressing herself. She had longed to have deep conversations with her friends and family, but few people understood and were as responsive as him. She enjoyed every bit of their discussion.

Even otherwise, they shared a lot in common. Abeera's brother and her friends made fun of her for drinking room temperature water or even putting the air conditioner of her room on 25 degrees and not 18 degrees like most people do. Antoine was identical. Everything was fitting right in place, just like a jigsaw puzzle.

Abeera was scared they might have a mind-to-mind argument. After all, she was familiar with men's egos, and her own. But there was not a single moment of ego in the relationship – just love that was naturally flowing between them, as if their souls had been longing to meet in physical bodies. Her heart was dancing with joy.

After they finished breakfast. They did their prayers in the mall and went back. In the afternoon, they went to a resort, Bab Al Shams. She was still in the "I love myself mode." It had taken her years to fall completely in love with herself and her freedom.

The resort was far away. They took a few hours to reach. After they reached they walked barefoot around the dunes, to the beach, to the poolside, and on the grass in the garden.

Was it another coincidence they both were wearing black? Black was Abeera's favorite *color. He looked like a model in his black shirt. She could hardly resist him. They spent a few hours walking, talking, smiling, and holding hands.*
They both said their evening prayers together before dinner. She came outside the prayer area and waited for him. They stared at the scenery, the beautiful and serene atmosphere, with its calmness, the voice of the waves of the sea dancing with the rhythm of her soul. Everything looked perfect and at peace.

A force was pushing her towards him, a strong desire to love him, to please him, to tell him she was completely his. He came outside the prayer hall. He held her hand, and they headed towards the restaurant for dinner. Abeera looked at the sky, the sparkling stars, and the moon shining, like diamonds in the sky and in her heart. It was wonderfully romantic.

They had dinner, Abeera shared with him her stories of how miserable it had been looking for a partner. She had felt alien all her life. He calmly listened to her stories.

After dinner they headed for tea and walked to the terrace. He held her hand in his hand again, and with every step Abeera took, she felt gratitude. She thanked God. It was as if the universe was dancing with her. It was mesmerizing; she felt like she was flying in the air, in the clouds, playing with the stars. The man she was walking with felt no less than an angel.

Abeera placed her head on his shoulder, looked at the stars, drank tea and couldn't help tears rolling down her cheeks in gratitude. He held her hand tightly and kissed her forehead.

Finally, she was physically with the sensuous man of her dreams. But it didn't matter. A glimpse of this lovely relationship with him was enough to uplift her soul.

Abeera felt a magnetic attraction between them. Her whole being was incredibly elated, *was Antoine actually "the man of my dreams?" Why do they call some people's soul mates? Is it because they are connected through souls? How did I connect with him so beautifully? I didn't need to resist anything, or worry about my past, my open mindedness, my looks, or about anything at all. He felt a part of me. I felt secure with him. I had fallen head over heels in love with this guy. The love between us had continued growing both physically and spiritually since the moment we connected.*

They talked for several hours again. Abeera told him, "I will always remember you and the special moments I have shared with you."

They walked for a while outside on the beach before leaving. It reminded her of all the romantic movies she had watched since she was young. Antoine's entire attention was just on her.

He kissed her again while they were heading back to the car. He put his arm around her. She enjoyed his beautiful scent and the calm aura of being with him, staring at the sky together, with the dim florescent light on the streets while they sat in the car. Driving towards home, they listened to romantic songs of the 80's.

That night, Abeera reviewed the entire day again in her mind. It was mesmerizing, magnificent, and a dream coming true. Her whole being was dancing and smiling joyously. Her heart and soul felt astounded by the dark night, the silence, the walk, the beach, the dunes, and the Divine remembrance deep within her heart and soul. She wrote:

Candlelight dinner!
The beach, the me, the him
Far from the mundane life
The silence, the romance
The shining moon and
The waves of the water
All synchronized with me and
My dancing heart
Candlelight dinner!

The second day they went to Atlantis, the palm. They said their evening prayers. The ambience was very peaceful. Antoine's presence had a very different effect on her. She was never this relaxed with anyone, even with some of her friends she often had her tantrums, but with him she was calm and composed. He was so concerned about her that he would make sure she smiled all the time. Whenever he saw the disappointments and frustrations of her terrible past on her face he immediately reminded her, "Smile, it is over. Be happy." For the first time in years, nothing else mattered to Abeera. In all her life Abeera had met nobody like him.

Abeera was so lost in him. She even forgot to take pictures with him. They fitted perfectly together. Abeera was bad with directions and he was so at ease with the navigator in the car. He would work out the route and she would drive to his directions. They complemented each other.

His tender kisses and gentle touch aroused her body. His touch was not an ordinary touch or the touch of an ordinary man. This was the touch of her soul and his soul. They were immensely fascinated that the love between them unfolded so naturally without the need to see each other or even speak to each other. They did not know the emails would miraculously bring them here one day. All the theories she had learned for playing hard to get had failed. Without recurring thoughts and logic, she had surrendered to this love that was finding its own way. It was magical.

A few days ago, she had to convince herself that this was something special. Every time she thought to write something in her next email, the next day his email would come with the same words she had in mind.

Abeera thought. When God plans for two souls to meet. Intuitions or telepathy everything looks small and everything comes together to bring them together. These were divine moments of being ecstatically wrapped in each other's arms. These moments were so beautiful. I don't seem to get enough of him.

Two days passed in Antoine's presence, and it seemed as if they had spent many years together.

He continued the conversation, "I understand awareness and consciousness. But for many people, it seems like a tall order or something very specific. Awareness is simply being aware of yourself, your habits, your thinking patterns, your mental health, your physical health etc., and consciousness is that state of your awareness. There are many levels, which is tricky and can cause confusion if one hasn't experienced it. If one has experienced it, then it's just a matter of words to explain it. But words are only pointers, and everyone has their own unique way to define it. I have become much more aware of myself during the last few years. I recognize that."

"It is the same for me. Ten years ago, I was completely different: an arrogant young girl." Abeera laughed.

"So, do you want to discuss your favorite subjects, God, love and relationships?"

"I am always ready for that."

"Everything is connected. Life, love, God, relationships and all there is."

"God is in all things and in every place. There is not a place in the world in which he is not most truly present."

"The first relationship one ever has is with oneself. The only person important is your own self. And when you give priority to yourself you give priority to God. When you love yourself, you love God, because an inward journey to self can lead to experience God's presence."

"Relationships are beautiful, but if used only as a 'means'. If you learn the art of using your relationships for their intended purpose, you will create magnificent relationships for yourself and the others surrounding."

"And for romantic relationships?" Antoine asked.

"Nothing changes. It is a very important 'means' for spiritual growth. Your spouse has more rights over you and you have more rights over them. That is the creation of God, the masculine and the feminine.

"But remember the first love of your life, as we call it when we are young: the stomach churning, the butterflies in the stomach, to stare at them for hours, to talk to them about their day-to-day life, and it never seems enough. We should strive to achieve that relationship and state with God, to live for God, to communicate with God, to share our routines with God, to enrich our relationship with God."

Antoine replied, "You mean to build that relationship when we as Muslims pray five times a day?"

"Exactly as you know it," Abeera smiled.

"Yes, but for most people, it's not as easy as we understand it."

"Yes, because there is a difference. It involves persistence, determination, and hard work to build your relationship with God. Our problem is that we want everything instantly. But the journey to God has bumps. It's not an easy ride, and many people give up, whereas with romantic love relationship, some people keep pursuing it for years and years."

"You are right," Antoine continued, "I understand. God loves us, but the question is: are we doing things to get His blessings, attention, and love? Are we investing in our relationship with God? When you love God truly, you will do things for His pleasure and refrain from things that will spoil your relationship with Him. God's mercy and love is there for everyone but are you turning to Him? That is the question."

"And the vows of marriage?"

"Well, the traditional vows are confusing to me."

"The correct vow should be: hand in hand, side by side, let's walk together in this life to God together. Both the partners promise to support each other for their individual and mutual purpose of lives together."

"We keep talking about the serious stuff in life." Antoine said and smiled.

"Actually, that has been my passion. Study yourself, and you will become a writer, an artist, a psychologist or whatnot. That's a study that involves everything." Abeera laughed. "So let's take a break and coming back to your question: how many boyfriends I had?"

"It's funny. According to my definition of relationships now, I guess the answer is 'None.' I was searching for that one man, and, actually in the search, I had met many men on my journey. It was adventurous sometimes; at least, that

The Spiritual Love

is what I thought. But, I learned a lot about myself. They were pointers when I reflected seriously. They helped me in developing love for myself, which I had neglected by being with them in the first place."

The relationship was becoming deeper and deeper. Their compatibility bewildered her.

Abeera danced with him. He lifted her in his arms and kissed her. A moment of wonderment again. She felt hypnotized: the tenderness of his lips, her heart racing and her breath increasing. Abeera got completely lost and excited in him. She wrote:

You and I
A dream coming true
I asked true love from God
And He sent me you
You are an angel
You are a Divine gift
I exist because you exist

At night they went to the seaside close by. Another night was spent in engaging, smiling, talking, and looking at the stars together.
Antoine told her, "You have a very special place in my heart. You are my princess." It was one of those happiest moments of her life, when she could see her soul dancing in excitement. She had longed to hear this. He reached her heart and touched her soul.

Abeera reviews the day again in her mind. In life you probably meet one person who you can talk with for hours and never feel bored, with whom you can share everything without being judged, with whom you can share your dark dingy secrets, your happiness, your sorrows, your good and bad, your desires and your fantasies. After meeting that person, you can never go back to who you were!

Abeera told him, "You are a tool for me to align myself with the desire that God has for me. I have been practicing alignment with myself this past few years. The momentum of my new 'me' was already building effortlessly. I could feel the new and unique version of myself. I had never thought I could love a man with such openness and non-judgments."

By now she had stopped beating the drum of, "I love myself."
Antoine teased her, "Where did that me, me (I love myself) go?" as if he had taken her most precious "herself" from here. She was completely speechless and bewildered.

Finally, it was the last day and she could hardly find the words to tell him what these days and nights had meant for her. In the end, it's all about the connection, the chemistry, the sharing, the caring, the love, and the understanding! They had coffee and her favorite Chinese cuisine.

They enjoyed their discussions and experiences again.

No wonder it was an automatic recognition and a blend of divine communion. "You are an amazing guy, indeed. I love you, I love you, and I love you," she whispered in his ears.

The last day, sitting on his lap, she kept repeating how good he was, how everything had changed in just a matter of few days how amazing it had been with him for the last few days. *Some relationships are so strong, beyond expression, so true, you don't even have to use the word "commitment" with them. You are committed to yourself and they are nothing other than a part of you. The image that I had sculpted in my dreams long ago was him!*

She whispered, "I am not scared to go to any lengths with you. My heart feels no separation. I love you. I love you, and 'I love you' seems so small."

And then it was time to say goodbye. Abeera told Antoine, "When you have memories in your heart, goodbyes are not goodbyes. We are connected in our thoughts and in our hearts."

He kissed her at the airport and whispered, *"You have carved your name on my heart and no one and nothing can replace that. I will wait forever to be with you. And from this moment on, I am all yours: my body, my heart, my soul and my mind. Will you marry me?"*

Abeera replied looking into his eyes, "Yes! I will! I will wait for you forever." This was an uplifting experience for both of them. She was waiting to have him completely.

Abeera thanked him and thanked God. She could not find words to express this magnificent relationship and the natural connection. She never thought God could send her an angel. It was an indescribable pleasure and the overwhelming feeling with this amazing guy. He was, gentle, patient and kind, his words – all put together – an angel in a human body.

Just a few months ago Abeera was lonely, resigned to being single, isolated in a bubble of independence and freedom, finding her alignment and God in everything, and here she was: she wanted to find her heart's desire but it ended up with Antoine.

Abeera looks at herself in the mirror and tells herself. Yes, God has answered my prayers. Yes, God responds to a heart that has faith. A heart to heart connection, a soul to soul connection, a connection beyond imagination. Yes, this relationship is a divine love connection: divinely protected, divinely planned, and divinely initiated. And the divine's timings are perfect to connect the two hearts to

The Spiritual Love

a deliberate purpose in life. I am inquisitive and excited to see how the path of life unfolds itself and how the journey of life is with Antoine.

I am no Juliet and he is no Romeo, yet God destined us to meet on the path of life and show ourselves how deserving and worthy we are of this love, that God has designed for us.

And who was planning all this? God. I am now his, madly, deeply, and totally. In my heart is immense love for him. Where does this come from? From God, in whom I put my trust.

Abeera wrote a poem:

Some people leave their heart prints in your life
Nobody can fill that empty space in your heart except them
I know nothing, neither have I attempted to know
Yet listen to my heart speaking, let it declare all it has to
It had lived more in 4 days than it ever had earlier
It seems as if it's happening, and I have no control over
Destiny might also be an undersized word, words stand short
The day my heart saw you, it only had one desire
Desire to know you, desire to love you!
A beautiful essence of you that my life is now revolving around
I close my eyes, I see you, with open eyes, I see you, it is just you everywhere.

THE GIRL WHO LOVED HERSELF

Lessons we can learn from Abeera:

Abeera spent 32 years seeking God and herself and then she not only found herself and God, but she also found a divine gift, a spiritual love, "Love yourself and love will come to you."

Indeed, if one has God's love, He will give you everything, and everything beyond measure.

No matter how educated you are, how rich or poor you are, black or white, beautiful or not, God loves you. All you must do is turn your attention to Him sincerely. Only He is your true friend, He is your true 'lover', and only He is all you want.

Abeera found God in darkness. She believed His love is so powerful that He will sort everything for her. True believers of God never give up. True believers always love God and love always wins. Love is powerful. Love is courageous. Love is strong.

Chapter 12

A New Beginning

We often forget that there are abundant resources in this universe. If we only trust God, we can have everything we want or even that which we have never desired.

Marriage and relationships had become frightening for Abeera. But here she was, immensely fascinated by this man, wondering, *is this how honeymoons are in reality?* They were lost in each other, a complete world to each other. Every day Antoine would take Abeera in his arms and she would not resist.

Spiritual love finds its own course. Finally, her desire for a lovely relationship was coming true. God had orchestrated a relationship. She had thought there was no man in this world she could trust. But despite all the abandonment from her loved ones, here she was, completely trusting Antoine beyond words and beyond all experiences of life.

This was God's will. No matter how much she worried and how much she tried to escape, this was it. They were poles apart and from two very different societies and upbringing, but there they were. They looked identical.

September 2016

Abeera shared Antoine's visit with her aunt who convinced Abeera, "God has sent a companion for you, an angel for you. God has answered your prayers."

Abeera realized God's plan for her was to marry Antoine Paris.

There were a few signs for Abeera before Antoine came to Dubai. She had no clue that God was finally rewarding her for all her patience, her struggles, and her faith.

The first sign, was the persuasion of her friend in Malaysia, the unexpected meeting, and the long talks they shared.

The second sign was in Ramadan when Abeera and Antoine were emailing each other, Abeera prayed, "God, please make it easier for me and Antoine." This was a real surprise for Abeera. All Abeera's prayers were asking for God. Although she was enjoying the emails, she didn't know it was God's plan bringing her and Antoine together.

The third and fourth sign was that Abeera's aunt and Amir were going back to Pakistan.

The fifth sign came when Abeera went for a massage and she didn't feel good about it. When the lady touched her, it felt very uncomfortable. This was another sign Abeera couldn't recognize, but any energy that interrupted the flow of the two of them was not a good feeling.

The sixth sign came when Samar proposed marriage to Abeera. But he felt she had completely changed and something was going on in her life. Abeera couldn't recognize it.

Abeera couldn't understand what was going on, but this was all interconnected with God's plan for her. When Antoine came to Dubai, everything was clear to her. The fact was that God was creating another opportunity for Abeera and Antoine to connect and experience their love for one another. That is how God's plan works, so one needs not to worry. When God plans something, everything comes together to make it happen and lead to beautiful memories.

Soon Antoine and Abeera decided on a date in the following month for their wedding in Dubai and invited their families.

October 2016

A traditional Pakistan wedding celebration lasts three to five days, or even more. Pakistani weddings consist of many customs and ceremonial events, from the engagement to the wedding day and a reception on the day after the wedding, and it does not end there. But Abeera and Antoine's wedding day was a beautiful day in its simplicity. They organized a simple event at Imran's place and then gathered for dinner with their guests at a restaurant.

Abeera had spent the day, like most brides, in the parlour. She was wearing a beige-colored Pakistani designer dress with a golden clutch and golden high heels. Necklace, earrings and a tikka (in the center of her forehead). Her curly hair beautifully done. On her hand she was wearing gold bangles. She looked gorgeous.

Antoine looked very handsome, wearing a grey suit with a white shirt, and a tie matching Abeera's beige dress.

Traditionally, there is a large procession led by the bridegroom, with a wedding band and entertainers, photographers and videographers, with displays of fireworks and accompanied by the rhythm of drums and music, to arrive at the wedding venue or the meeting point, where most or all the family members of the bride meet and greet.

Under the Islamic Shariah/law, a formal contract, which is considered an integral and valid part of an Islamic religious marriage, outlines the responsibilities and rights of the bridegroom and the bride, and an agreed document (which is for everyone) is signed in the Nikah (marriage) ceremony. In the presence of at least two witnesses, the bridegroom and bride both repeat the word "Qabul" (in English: I accept her/him as wife/husband) three times, then a government-authorized registrar completes all the documents, to be registered in the government records.

Abeera was sitting in a covered area with her mother, aunt and friends before the ceremony of acceptance was performed. She signed the documents and accepted the proposal. The contract of marriage was signed by Antoine and Abeera, and then Abeera's cousin Eman distributed the traditional sweets. Abeera was then taken to the room where she could now sit with the bridegroom and have photographs taken with the guests.

Antoine was sitting with his father, Abeera's father and all the male guests.

Her cousin Eman, meanwhile, distributed gifts to all the people who attended the wedding ceremony. This was followed by the traditional ceremony of feeding flavoured milk to the bridegroom which was done by Abeera's cousin Eman.

THE GIRL WHO LOVED HERSELF

The guest presented gifts to the couple. The bridegroom gave a beautiful wedding ring to the bride, and then the couple headed to the opposite side of the lounge for the cake cutting ceremony. The function ended after dinner which was arranged at a Pakistani restaurant. Abeera had organized a simple occasion and fulfilled all her small wishes.

After the dinner, Abeera and Antoine thanked all the guests and spent the first two nights in a hotel in Jumeirah.

The next night, they went out for dinner with her parents-in-law. Abeera couldn't believe it when her mother-in-law held her hand and said, "I love you because my son loves you." Abeera looked at her husband in astonishment. He smiled and gave her a sign to relax and not cry.

The second night of the marriage Abeera's family took the couple and her in-laws out for dinner.

The third night. The bride and the groom checked out and then celebrated a few nights in a lovely resort, far from the hustle and bustle of city life in Ras Al Khaimah (UAE).

Soon it was time for Antoine to travel back to London.

After a few months of the wedding. Antoine got the paperwork for Abeera and invited her to London. They went for the reception from Antoine's parents to France and then celebrated honeymoon in Italy and Switzerland.

Another dream of Abeera was now coming true: visiting Europe with her husband.

Abeera was singing, dancing, and taking pictures, enjoying her honeymoon in Europe.

She would often think while staring at the boats, beach, the mountains, and the natural beauty about all the hardships she had gone through to be here where she was. But it was worth it. In the end, Abeera not only found God and answers to all her questions, but God also rewarded her with this new relationship.

Abeera didn't stop writing poems to her husband till she joined him permanently in London.

My silly heart
Wants to keep reminding you
I love you I love you I love you
In the day, in the night
In the morning, in the evening
In every hour, in every minute
In every second of the day

A New Beginning

My silly heart
Wants to keep sharing
Share every part of me
The today, the yesterday,
The future
The secrets of my past
The desires of my future
The good, the bad
The right, the wrong
Every phase of my life with you

My silly heart wants to keep
Thinking of you, missing you
Kiss you, touch you
Feel you, love you
Taste you, eat you,

My silly heart wants to
Feel your breath inside me
Wants you so close
Where I can lose myself
And get lost in you.

My silly heart wants to know
Your every flaw
Your every perfection
Your every mistake
Your yesterday, your today
Your desires
Wants all of you

My silly heart wants you
In the laughter, in the sadness
In the summer, in the spring
In the darkness, in the light
In life, in the hereafter

THE GIRL WHO LOVED HERSELF

My silly heart desires to be with you
My silly heart is obsessed with you
My silly heart is fascinated with you
And my heart loves you for the will of God.

Abeera had transcended beautifully. The void she was trying to fill through relationships was the void within herself. That void nobody else could fill but herself, only the love of her soul and the love of her heart.

Soon it was time for Abeera to move to London. At first, Abeera resisted and panicked. She didn't want to leave her independence, Dubai, and her lovely job. But when God calls you, God prepares your heart and gives you ample time to prepare yourself.

Abeera's new life was waiting for her, with new goals, new challenges, new people, and a new country.

Abeera's every little wish was fulfilled, even her wish for her long hair. Now, her hair was growing long and beautiful.

She moved to London. London was a blessing, with beautiful weather, lots of rain and snow. Abeera had always loved the rain. Often, she would go out dressed up in her Pakistani attire and high heels on the streets of London with her husband and walk in the rain with an umbrella and sing many romantic songs. Abeera's wardrobe was filled with designer, heavily embroidered clothes of different colors and different styles, matching shoes and matching designer handbags. Abeera had learned to spend her money on herself rather than fulfilling the needs of others and providing for them.

Abeera wrote a thank you letter to God:

Dear God,
Thank you God, thank you very --- very much.
Take everything from me but never take this love of You that I have found.
The heart that is filled with Your love. Never take this feeling away from me.
Now, my life is complete. I have lost nothing. I have regained. I have regained it.

Thank you for setting me free.
My soul is rejoicing in love for You.
My heart is dancing in your love.
I am touched, I am bewildered.
I am intoxicated with your love.
Thank you God, thank you very --- very much.

Wrapped with love of my soul,
Abeera

Abeera's sister Savera called her again when she moved to London. She congratulated Abeera for moving to London. By this time Ameen and Nigar were already divorced. Moiz and his wife were also divorced. Savera told her she was diagnosed with brain tumor and her body was suffering.

So Savera was ill.

Savera told Abeera, "Today I want to declare that my husband Sohail is responsible for the two divorces in the family. He is also responsible for breaking your ties with dad."

Abeera was shocked. She replied, "But why would he do that?"

Savera added, "Please hold on, let me finish. It is not only him, but it is also because of me that dad abandoned you and abused you. It is because of us that dad betrayed you, lied to you and insulted you. The last time dad spoke to you when he abused you, we all were around. Sohail and I had always been jealous of you. We hated your freedom. We hated your relationship with dad, so we convinced dad to control you. To throw you out. The first time he asked you to leave was also because of us. And the second time he abused you was because we had convinced him he is the father and he has the right to do anything. We convinced him you were very emotional, and he should never get papers signed in your name. We scared him that the day Abeera gets the papers of the house in her name she will kick you out of the house and they will have nowhere else to go. Our mean-spirited planning endlessly fuelled dad's confrontation."

"But not only that. We were jealous of Moiz's wife. She knew we were jealous of her. And we wanted Moiz to control her. But Moiz failed to do so. Every time they fought, we used it as an opportunity to break their marriage. Finally, we could get them divorced."

"We broke Nigar's family also because Sohail wanted to be the only son-in-law getting respect, love, and control over our family."

"Our jealousy and insecurity had really broken the family and look where I am today struggling with the tumor. I never stood up for what was right. I always supported my husband because I was scared that if I went against him, he would divorce me. Please forgive me. I am ashamed. I don't know how to apologize. I remember you had tried hard to keep the family together. But after you moved to Dubai everything changed. Sohail ruled the family, and the family relationships broke."

Abeera smiled on the phone. She knew how miserable her life was in Lahore because of Sohail and Savera. But she had not expected that they would go to this extent.

Abeera calmly replied, "Don't be upset. Nothing can happen without the will of God. It was a test for me and tests are usually difficult. If it was easy, it won't be a test. We look for unconditional love in our relationships but in truth unconditional love is only for God. None of our relationships are perfect. Only God is perfect."

"With dad's abuse, I finally learned how to respect myself. The respect I had longed for; the courage I wanted to shine through me all my life. I learned that I don't have to put up with his disrespect. I learned to let go. I learned to let go the love I was holding so dearly. It was not love, it was command and reassurance. I took so long to accept that."

"With the physical violence, selfishness, and inconsiderate behavior of Moiz I learned how to stop being a victim. If he would have loved me, he would have never insulted me, hurt me, or beat me."

"It was me who was showering my love on the men of my family who didn't deserve my love. I was so madly in love with these relationships that had to fall apart one day. And you are making yourself responsible rather I want to thank you to have made my life easier to accept the truth."

"And with all this I became spiritual. To experience the love of God because every time I felt alone, sad, and depressed I turned to God. Maybe my relationships won't go back to where they were, but I have no regrets. I lost nothing. God compensated me beautifully. He gave me a new family in the shape of my in-laws. They adore me, I adore them. God has abundant resources but only for those who turn to Him. I am never alone. My faith in God increased so much that today I have everything I had ever dreamed of. God fulfilled all my dreams. God is the biggest Compensator. Indeed, I should rather be thankful to you all. You should also turn to God. I forgive you all. May God forgive you."

"And the man I am married to is a very different man. He doesn't know what dominating and controlling is. I learned from him equality, respect, sharing, and love in relationships. I have never seen this love in my family."

"It is only because of you all that I could understand the truth of relationships. The truth of self and the truth of God. Every relationship is meant to fail. The truth is that every relationship will fail you. Because that is not the truth."

"But if you accept and surrender to the will of God. God will provide you with the smallest and the biggest desire you ever had. But that can only happen if you accept and surrender to the will of God."

"I will pray that God gives health and prosperity to you and the family. I will pray that God helps the family and everyone turns to God for help."

"The only thing that ever matters is your relationship with God. Everything and every relationship is temporary and will fail you. Only God will never fail you."

"It was a dark phase of my soul. I had nowhere else to go. I asked God for mercy. I asked God for strength and look how miracles happened in my life. I found everything when I surrendered and submitted myself to the will of God."

Savera was crying. Abeera could only pray and have compassion for her and requested her to ask God for forgiveness.

Abeera ended the call by thanking her for sharing the burden she had on her heart.

Soon she travelled again to France and stayed with her in-laws. Abeera had always wanted a loving, caring, and sincere family. Now she had one; her soul was crying for how abundance can flow into your life when you submit and surrender yourself to God and accept your life and yourself.

Although she had to let go of her two relationships who she loved the most, her father and her brother, in reality, she was given a new family, a new love.

Her mother-in-law was not only caring but loving, very supportive, and always praised her, including her long hair, her clothes, and every little thing about Abeera. She would take care of the smallest of things for Abeera from shampoos to milk, from tea to halal meat, from shopping to gifts, etc.

It wasn't long before Abeera shared her personal story with her mother-in-law. She smiled and told Abeera, "Now you live in London with my son and nobody will trouble you. London is a free city. Enjoy your life as much as you can, and if you ever need us, don't hesitate. You are our daughter, and now I know why I never had a daughter because God had planned to send you as a daughter to us. You are a lovely daughter. We love you. You can visit us whenever you want and stay with us as long as you want, we are your family. We love you."

Antoine's grandma was also so welcoming. She was an independent, loving, and caring woman. Abeera stayed with her for a while. Grandma would translate French into English through a software and then talk to Abeera. Abeera was very pleased with Grandma's love and care. Grandma would buy chocolates and gifts for Abeera and often play cards with her.

Abeera was mesmerized with these beautiful relationships.

Soon, Abeera became a famous writer. Her friends, in-laws, ex-colleagues, teachers, classmates, everyone was proud of her—except her family, who thought she was egoistic and proud of herself by becoming an author, that she no longer cared about her parents and the family. But Abeera had tried hard not to break these relationships but every time they would lie to her and then insult her. Abeera finally left these relationships behind.

Pakistan, Dubai, London, Europe, Malaysia. Abeera couldn't believe her love story could be like that of a movie. A Pakistani lady living in Dubai met a French in Malaysia, who lived in London, fell in love and got married.

THE GIRL WHO LOVED HERSELF

Did they bring five countries together? Yes, everything is possible. This was Abeera's journey of self-love, courage and surrender.

Abeera wrote a poem: titled Dance, dance, dance

Every fiber of my body is on gratitude
Everything is dancing
Thank you, God

My destination is You
To whom I shall come always
Thank you, God

My heart dances with the beat around me
The world around me dances
Thank you, God

I am not scared of the storms
As long as I have you
Thank you, God

I am not worried about heaven and the hell
Let me sink in this intoxication of your love
Thank you, God

A New Beginning

Lessons we can learn from Abeera:

God tests us through our relationships, challenges us, only for us to understand the truth.

The relationship with God is that of faith, trust, and surrender.

Faith is irrational, and when you put faith in God, your perceptions of love, life, and God change. Faith has immense power, when you have faith in God, God never leaves you.

God always chooses the best for you. There is abundant wealth, resources, love, happiness, relationships, and all that one ever needs.

God can fulfill all your dreams and hopes only if you surrender to God.

When you leave your matters to God. God sorts everything beautifully.

God loves you. It is only a question of: do you love Him?
Do you look up to Him more than anyone?
Do you still believe in Him when everything is falling?
Do you still trust that God will take care of you?
Do you believe in the miracles of God?
Bless your life, no matter where it is, and let God guide you.
Find yourself first and then find God.

The only reason you would do something or not do it should be the same: will it affect my relationship with God? Will it strengthen my relationship with God?

Love yourself is the beginning of the journey that will lead you to the ultimate truth.

Sometimes you have to go through the thorns, the disappointments, the failures, as amongst of all this is life, life itself.

The test of lives are only a grander opening to get closer to God.

Only a burning heart finds God.

Have patience. If one chapter of your life has darkness, don't give in. The next chapter of your life could be that of light.

Life is an intimate and *sacred love story between you and God.*

www.ingramcontent.com/pod-product-compliance
Lightning Source LLC
Chambersburg PA
CBHW030522080526
44586CB00011B/289